Developing Traum: Approaches to Student Discipline

MW00795074

Building on comprehensive research conducted in US schools, this accessible volume offers an effective model of school leadership to develop and implement school-wide, trauma-responsive approaches to student discipline.

Recognizing that challenging student behaviors are often rooted in early experiences of trauma, the volume builds on a model from the Substance Abuse and Mental Health Services Administration (SAMHSA), to walk readers through the processes of realizing, recognizing, responding to, and resisting the impacts of trauma in school contexts. Research and interviews model an educational reform process and explain how a range of differentiated interventions including Positive Behavior Interventions and Supports (PBIS), social-emotional learning (SEL), restorative justice, and family engagement can be used to boost student resilience and pro-social behavior. Practical steps are supported by current theory, resources, and stories of implementation from superintendents, principals, and teachers.

This text will benefit school leaders, teachers, and counselors with an interest in restorative student discipline, emotional and behavioral difficulties in young people, and PreK-12 education more broadly. Those interested in school psychology, trauma studies, and trauma counseling with children and adolescents will also benefit from the volume.

Kirk Eggleston is Principal of Gayton Elementary School, Virginia, USA.

Erinn J. Green is Assistant Principal of Prince Edward County Elementary School, Virginia, USA.

Shawn Abel is Principal of Midlothian High School, Virginia, USA.

Stephanie Poe is Principal of Hopewell High School, Virginia, USA.

Charol Shakeshaft is Professor of Educational Leadership at Virginia Commonwealth University, USA.

Routledge Research in Education

This series aims to present the latest research from right across the field of education. It is not confined to any particular area or school of thought and seeks to provide coverage of a broad range of topics, theories and issues from around the world.

Recent titles in the series include:

For a complete list of titles in this series, please visit www.routledge.com/ Routledge-Research-in-Education/book-series/SE0393

Developing Trauma-Responsive Approaches to Student Discipline

A Guide to Trauma-Informed Practice in PreK-12 Schools

Kirk Eggleston, Erinn J. Green, Shawn Abel, Stephanie Poe, and Charol Shakeshaft

Routledge
Taylor & Francis Group

NEW YORK AND LONDON

First published 2021
by Routledge
605 Third Avenue, New York, NY 10158

and by Routledge
2 Park Square, Milton Park, Abingdon, Oxon, OX14 4RN

Routledge is an imprint of the Taylor & Francis Group, an informa business

Library of Congress Cataloging-in-Publication Data
A catalog record for this title has been requested

ISBN: 9780367651589 (hbk)
ISBN: 9780367651602 (pbk)
ISBN: 9781003128137 (ebk)

Typeset in Times New Roman
by Deanta Global Publishing Services, Chennai, India

Contents

Figures

Acknowledgments

We are grateful we were given the opportunity to partner with Greater Richmond Stop Child Abuse Now (GR-SCAN) to respond to the need for more trauma-responsive resources for Virginia school leaders. Our research has transformed the way we lead educators in our buildings and across the state to improve student outcomes. The most fulfilling part of the process was connecting with educators across the Commonwealth of Virginia who are implementing trauma-responsive practices. Every interview revealed a connection to another person or school invested in reforming traditional discipline practices to support the whole child. We are inspired by the transformational leaders we encountered on our journey. Thank you for sharing with us.

Greater Richmond Stop Child Abuse Now (GR-SCAN)
Margo Buchanan, RPS Resiliency Project Coordinator; *Melissa McGinn,* Community Programs Coordinator and Coordinator of GR-Trauma Informed Community Network; *Fred Orelove,* Volunteer; *Denise Powers,* Director and Teacher, Circle Preschool; *Olivya Wilson,* RPS Resiliency Project Parent Engagement coordinator
Virginia Commonwealth University
Barbara Driver, Assistant Professor; *Joshua Cole,* Executive Director, Office of Strategic Engagement
Charlottesville City Schools
Patrick Farrell, Behavior Support Specialist; *Shelia Sparks,* Coordinator of Preschool
Clark Elementary
Linda Anderson, Classroom Aide; *Pat Barbara,* Teacher; *Kelly Bullock,* Teacher; *Dana Carrico,* Teacher; *Kathryn Grant,* Teacher; *Linda Humphreys,* Instructional Coach; *Deanna Isley,* Principal
Chesterfield County Public Schools

Connie Honsinger, Intervention and Training Specialist, Trauma-Informed Care

Ecoff Elementary School

Margaret Ebbs, Teacher; *Bridget Manuel*, Teacher; *Renee Shimko-Daye*, Assistant Principal; *Kelsey Taylor*, Teacher; *Natalie Watts*, School Counselor

Fauquier County Public Schools

Carolyn Lamm, Supervisor of Student Support Services

Taylor Middle School

Whitney Boring, Assistant Principal; *Jeanine Ebson*, FAR Room Teacher; *Jennifer Linthicum*, Teacher & VTSS School-based Coach; *Trina Mikelonas*, Teacher & VTSS Data Lead; *Karen Pearson*, Former FAR Room Teacher; *Trina Roof,* School Counselor

Cedar Lee Middle School

Diane Graves, Special Education Teacher; *Leah Shorb*, Assistant Principal

Verdun Adventure Bound

Honore Hastings, Executive Director; *Sean McElhinney*, Challenge Course Manager and Lead Facilitator

Mental Health Association of Fauquier

Sally Morgan, Executive Director; *John Waldeck*, Special Project Coordinator

Piedmont Dispute Resolution

Lawrie Parker, Founder and Executive Director

CADRE

Kathleen Weghorst, Executive Director

Harrisonburg County Public Schools

Bethany Everidge, Career and Technical Education Coordinator

Henrico County Public Schools

Nyah Hamlett, Assistant Superintendent for Instructional Support; *William Noel, Sr.*, Director of Student Support and Disciplinary Review

Loudoun County Public Schools

Lisa Fillipovich, Coordinator of Positive Behavior Interventions and Supports; *John Lody*, Director of Diagnostic and Prevention Services in the Department of Pupil Services; *Jennifer Wall*, LPC, Supervisor of Student Assistance Services in the Department of Pupil Services; *Eric Williams*, Superintendent

Richmond Public Schools

Ram Bhagat, Manager of School Culture and Climate Strategy; *Angela Jones,* Director of Culture, Climate, & Student Services

Fairfax County Parent Advocate

Jenna White, PTA Council Liaison to the Trauma-Informed Community Network

Virginia Department of Education

Sophia Farmer, Lead VTSS Implementation Specialist; *Maribel Saimre*, Director of Student Services; *Michael Crusco*, VTSS Systems Change Coach; *Kim Dupre*, VTSS Systems Change Coach; *Anna Hebb*, VTSS Systems Change Coach; *Wendi Jenkins*, VTSS Systems Change Coach

Garrity Mediation and Counseling

Bob Garrity, Consultant

Virginia Center for Inclusive Communities

Jessica Hawthorne, Director of Programs

ChildSavers

John Richardson-Lauve, Director of Mental Health

Integration Solutions Inc.

Allison Sampson-Jackson, CEO

Bare Soul Yoga

Ashley Williams, Owner & Founder

About the Authors

Kirk Eggleston, EdD, taught middle school English eight years in public and private schools in Washington, DC, and four years at an international school in Quito, Ecuador. For the last 18 years he has served as an administrator in Henrico County, Virginia. He has been principal of three elementary schools with diverse student and community needs. Restorative discipline has been an essential component of his educational philosophy throughout his career. Eggleston earned his BA at the College of William & Mary, Master of Education Leadership from George Mason University, and Doctor of Education in Leadership from Virginia Commonwealth University.

Erinn J. Green, EdD, began her educational career as a group counselor at a residential therapeutic wilderness school for youth. She transitioned into public schools as a special education teacher and later served as a systems change coach at the Virginia Department of Education's Training and Technical Assistance Center at Virginia Commonwealth University. In July 2019, Green began her current role as an assistant principal in Prince Edward County Public Schools in Farmville, Virginia. Green has dedicated her career to supporting students, families, and educators with improving outcomes of students with unique learning, behavioral, and social-emotional needs. Green earned her BA at the University of Michigan, Master of Special Education K–12 from Longwood University, and Doctor of Education in Leadership at Virginia Commonwealth University.

Shawn Abel, EdD, began his educational career in 1996 as a secondary math and computer teacher. He served as an assistant principal from 2005 to 2012. In 2012, Abel accepted the calling of principal at Midlothian High School in Chesterfield County, Virginia. Over the past several years, Abel has conducted extensive research in an effort to provide an equitable and inclusive education for all students. Abel earned his BS in Business and

Math Education at Buffalo State University and both Master and Doctor of Education in Leadership from Virginia Commonwealth University.

Stephanie Poe, EdD, has over 30 years of experience in education. Poe taught high school science and was a technology resource teacher before becoming a school administrator. She is currently the principal of Hopewell High School in Hopewell, Virginia. Poe earned her BS in biology from Longwood University, an MA in curriculum and instruction from Virginia Tech, and a Doctor of Education in Leadership at Virginia Commonwealth University. Poe is passionate about working with students of diverse backgrounds. She utilizes trauma-responsive practices and resilience strategies to support students, parents, and teachers.

Charol Shakeshaft, PhD, is professor of Educational Leadership at Virginia Commonwealth University. She has been studying equity in schools for over three decades. She was elected an AERA fellow in 2015 and received the 2015 AERA Distinguished Contributions to Gender Equity in Education Research Award and the 2020 AERA Lifetime Award for Research. She is the author of three books and over 200 refereed articles and papers. Dr. Shakeshaft served as Capstone advisor of this doctoral research in the Virginia Commonwealth University Department of Educational Leadership.

Preface
A Synthesis of Solutions

Greater Richmond Stop Child Abuse Now (GR-SCAN) is a non-profit child advocacy organization serving Richmond, Virginia, and surrounding counties. Five GR-SCAN programs are designed to support children and families. These include the Family Support Program, Community Programs, the Circle Preschool Program, Richmond Court Appointed Special Advocates (CASA), and the Child Advocacy Centers. The Greater Richmond Trauma-Informed Community Network (GR-TICN), also convened by GR-SCAN, is a diverse group of 385 members from 160 different public, private, non-profit, state, and local government agencies who share a commitment to a more trauma-informed and resilient community. The GR-TICN provides training to schools about the effects of adverse childhood experiences (ACEs) and toxic stress on student learning and behavior.

In 2017, GR-SCAN received requests from surrounding Virginia school divisions for trauma-informed alternatives to suspensions. Annual suspensions were high statewide, disproportionately affecting Black students, students with disabilities (SWD), and students living in poverty. The Virginia General Assembly had recently passed new state laws that limited the length of time for which a student could be suspended and prohibited long-term suspension and expulsion of students in pre-kindergarten through third grade. While these laws created a sense of urgency for reformed discipline practices, school divisions had few practical alternatives to suspension. Greater Richmond Stop Child Abuse Now solicited support from Virginia Commonwealth University's (VCU) School of Education to research the use of trauma-responsive discipline practices in schools and to make recommendations for policy and professional resources for school leaders.

Under the supervision of Dr. Charol Shakeshaft, PhD, in VCU's Department of Educational Leadership, a Capstone team of EdD students was assigned to conduct the research. In May 2018, doctoral candidates Kirk Eggleston, Erinn J. Green, Shawn Abel, and Stephanie Poe began a partnership with GR-SCAN. As school administrators, they shared a common belief that student behavior communicates needs and student discipline is an opportunity to teach versus an obligation to punish. Their research showed that trauma-responsive discipline requires a fundamental shift in mindset from zero-tolerance to restorative practices. For this reason, the Capstone team synthesized its research into a leadership guide for GR-SCAN to assist Virginia schools and divisions with transformational reform.

This book is an adaptation of the original product. The authors use Virginia as a case study to illustrate a national problem of exclusionary discipline. The goal of this guide is to inform and empower educational leaders in every state to implement trauma-responsive discipline practices. The authors thank GR-SCAN for their continued partnership and Routledge Press for publishing and distributing this book to a wide audience of educators who aspire to make a difference with all children.

Introduction

Examining the Purpose of Student Discipline

When a student, Miguel, is struggling to read or solve a math problem, his teacher, Ms. Smith, responds by reteaching the skill. She may take an alternate approach, explain further, illustrate, model, review, practice, and assess once again. She may employ a personal connection or inject humor to make the concept more relevant, and Miguel's act of trying again (and yet again) is less of an emotional risk. Ms. Smith may also look for additional resources, parent assistance, and/or refer him for intervention; she will not give up on Miguel because she is a teacher and he is her student. Finally, at that moment when Miguel does demonstrate "he gets it," Ms. Smith will celebrate the victory with him, his mother, and the principal. She will feel proud and effective having empowered Miguel with the skills and resilience to meet the next challenge.

By Ms. Smith's model, learning is how we measure the quality of every teacher's instruction and ingenuity in the classroom. So when another student, Daniel, is struggling to behave, sit in his seat, or comply with classroom expectations, why do we readily accept a different response? According to Ms. Smith, Daniel's conduct is not a skill deficit but an obvious choice to be bad.

> Daniel should know right from wrong. His outburst was deliberate, and so he must move his name to the yellow warning sign at the front of the classroom. When he misbehaves again, he will need to move his name to the red stop sign and have a more serious consequence—10 minutes walking alone around the track at recess. The next time it will be 15 minutes of recess, then 20. It is no wonder Daniel isn't learning. He is always misbehaving, refusing to work, playing the class clown, testing my will against his. Daniel is just not worth the effort if his mother is not going to do anything about his behavior. The other students are suffering as a result of my instructional time wasted on him.

If Daniel cannot follow the classroom rules, he will receive a referral to the principal's office. The threat is real, and soon Daniel is down the hall and out of Ms. Smith's classroom.

What happens next is up to the principal, and the focus of our book. As school administrators with decades of experience between us, we appreciate the dichotomy between classroom instruction and classroom discipline. While Ms. Smith invests herself tirelessly to differentiate for the compliant child, she can be quick to abdicate her authority with the defiant one. Most likely, Ms. Smith believes that the principal will back her up by punishing Daniel more. That is what she and her colleagues have come to expect from the principal. Corporal punishment in public schools is still legal in 19 states (Walker, 2016). Even where it is banned the principal's perceived role is still as the one who carries the stick. Wielding the stick in the teacher's favor means the principal should punish Daniel enough to set him straight and make him an example to his classmates. Not wielding the stick in the teacher's favor means being seen as "weak on discipline" and unsupportive of the teacher. In other words, what the principal determines for Daniel has become most pressingly about Ms. Smith, her colleagues, and the principal's own reputation in the building.

We believe that what the principal determines for Daniel must be all about Daniel. Daniel's father is in jail and his mother works two jobs. As a six-year old, Daniel watched his mother get beaten, and Daniel continues to suffer from nightmares and separation anxiety. His behavior at school is not always a choice and is often a natural response to a classroom management plan that makes Daniel feel increasingly anxious and singled out. A day of in-school suspension will likely not teach Daniel discipline. A day of out-of-school suspension will damage any trust developed between the school and Daniel's mother, and could have the potential to traumatize Daniel further. Shaming Daniel and sending him back to class to recover whatever instruction and social standing he has lost is not going to help him, either.

Bringing Daniel back to the classroom and working directly with him and his teacher will help him greatly. Daniel will most benefit from a positive intervention school-home support plan coordinated together with Ms. Smith and his mother. Checking in and out with Daniel every morning and afternoon will strengthen and reward his personal accountability. Coaching Ms. Smith to foster a relationship with Daniel will make a critical difference in how he sees himself and how he interacts respectfully with her and his classmates. Challenging Ms. Smith to teach Daniel discipline like she teaches reading and math will further boost her self-efficacy as a teacher of Daniel and many students like him.

We believe the principal's mandate is to lead a paradigm shift of discipline practice with every teacher in the building. According to Merriam

Webster (2020), *discipline* is a verb with two distinct meanings: *(1) to punish or penalize for the sake of enforcing obedience and perfecting moral character; (2) to train or develop by instruction and exercise especially in self-control.* The goal of this book is to help educational leaders redefine school discipline from the first to second definition—from wielding discipline as a punishment to teaching discipline as a process of instruction and a product of social and emotional health for *all* students. Educational leaders include superintendents, directors, specialists, principals, assistant principals, deans, teachers, instructional assistants, support staff, custodians, cafeteria workers, bus drivers, parents, consultants, volunteers, and students.

Leading a paradigm shift of discipline practice will amount to a culture change in many schools. Transformational leadership requires urgency, vision, strategy, and systematization, an intentional and sequential process of buy-in that brings people and progress together (Kotter, 2019). We have divided the book into two sections to guide this process. Part I: Understanding the Need for Trauma-Responsive Discipline Reform provides a rationale for change. Chapter 1 identifies exclusionary discipline as a system that is punitive, racially biased, poverty sustaining, and contributing to childhood trauma. Chapter 2 summarizes the brain science of adverse childhood experiences (ACEs), trauma, and resilience, and justifies why we should view student discipline through a trauma-informed lens. Chapter 3 recommends that leaders within schools and school divisions utilize our *Discipline Reform Model*, and appeals for local and state legislators to fund trauma-informed systems and supports.

Part II: Leading Trauma-Responsive Discipline Reform details steps to effect change. We sequence these chapters using a research-based model, the Substance Abuse and Mental Health Services Administration (SAMHSA)'s four **R**s of how to support individuals impacted by trauma. Chapter 4, **R**ealize, helps to develop a schoolwide awareness of trauma by creating a sense of urgency and developing a guiding coalition for change. Chapter 5, **R**ecognize, establishes an acknowledgment of trauma in the school context and guides the creation and communication of a restorative vision of discipline. Chapter 6, **R**espond, provides an overview of specific trauma-responsive practices and offers suggestions for implementing them. Chapter 7, **R**esist, offers ways to avoid re-traumatization, sustain momentum, and build student resilience in all children with trauma-informed systems and supports. The Epilogue identifies the urgency for trauma-responsive discipline reform in the context of COVID-19 school closures and their disproportionate impact on Black children.

We hope this book will help build guiding coalitions of educational leaders across the nation with visions for empowering change. We identify successful practices, tell school-based stories, share a synthesis of recommendations, and provide professional development resources. Our highlights of school initiatives and interviews with experts provide a clear picture of how trauma-responsive practices can be implemented across school settings to teach and support student discipline. We do not claim to present a comprehensive account of the trauma-responsive work currently conducted in US public schools. Rather, we have provided a representation of practitioners and experts in the Commonwealth of Virginia serving urban, suburban, and rural school divisions. We describe their various initiatives, PreK-12, that can be replicated in all 50 states. Divisions and schools were selected based on their proactive and successful approaches to trauma-responsive practices. Individual experts also contributed valuable insight in defining what it means to become a trauma-informed school. The sum of experts and school initiatives together offers recommendations on how to develop student resilience and responsibility through trauma-responsive discipline.

We want to thank each of our interviewees for their valuable contribution to our research and to the process of trauma-responsive discipline reform taking place in school communities across the country. One division leader we interviewed likened the process to eating an elephant. "It's so hard to know where to start!"

Together we start here.

References

Kotter International. (2019). *Kotter*. Retrieved from https://www.kotterinc.com/8-st eps-process-for-leading-change/.

Merriam Webster. (2020). Retrieved from https://www.merriam-webster.com/dic tionary/Discipline.

Walker, T. (2016). Why are 19 states still allowing corporal punishment in schools? *NEA Today*. Retrieved from https://www.nea.org/advocating-for-change/new -from-nea/Why-are-19-states-still-allowing-corporal-punishment-schools.

Part I
Understanding the Need for Trauma-Responsive Discipline Reform

1 Identifying the Problems of Exclusionary Discipline

According to the National Clearinghouse on Supportive School Discipline, *exclusionary discipline* is any form of school disciplinary action "that removes or excludes a student from his or her usual educational setting" (Exclusionary Discipline, 2018). Exclusionary discipline ranges from an hour in the principal's office, to several hours of in-school suspension, to a day or more suspended out of school, to an entire year of expulsion from school. Over the last 30 years, exclusionary discipline has been widely practiced in schools throughout the United States in accordance with *zero-tolerance* policies. These policies mandate predetermined consequences for specific offenses under the presumption that strict enforcement of rules is an effective deterrent to breaking them (Lhamon et al., 2019).

Originally intended to reduce violence in schools, zero-tolerance policies have extended the use of exclusionary discipline "to an ever-widening range of infractions, including serious incidents (e.g., weapons, fighting) to lesser infractions (e.g., wearing hats, failing to complete homework)" (Lhamon et al., 2019, p. 28). As early as 2001, the American Bar Association condemned zero-tolerance policies for being "a one-size-fits-all solution to all the problems that schools confront," redefining "students as criminals," eliminating "the common sense that comes with discretion," and doing "little to improve school safety" (National Child Traumatic Stress Network, 2018). Despite such criticism, zero-tolerance policies have continued to justify a system of student discipline that is punitive, racially biased, poverty sustaining, and contributing to childhood trauma.

Exclusionary Discipline is a Punitive System

In Virginia, where four of us serve as principals, zero-tolerance policies have until recently been the norm, and out-of-school forms of discipline are the penalty principals have practiced most commonly (Langberg & Ciolfi, 2016; Woolard, 2017). In May 2016, Legal Aid Justice Center first published *Suspended Progress*, an annual review of discipline data reported by local

Virginia school divisions to the Virginia Department of Education (VDOE). The report identified approximately 70,000 individual students who had been issued over 126,000 out-of-school suspensions (OSS) as punishment for code of conduct violations during the 2014–2015 school year (Langberg & Ciolfi, 2016). *Suspended Progress* broke down the data further by school levels, school divisions, types of offenses, and demographics as follows:

> Over 20% of suspensions were issued to elementary school students, including 16,000 suspensions to students in pre-kindergarten through third grade. Over 10% of ninth grade students were suspended at least once. In seven divisions, more than 15% of all students were suspended at least once. The majority of suspensions were issued for non-violent, relatively minor misbehavior. In fact, approximately half of suspensions were for cell phone use, disruption, defiance, insubordination, and disrespect. Perhaps counterintuitively, 670 suspensions were issued for attendance. In other words, students were suspended from school for skipping class or not coming to school. (Langberg & Ciolfi, 2016, para 2–3)

Legal Aid Justice Center has provided updates annually since the original report. In 2016–2017, the most recent data available, suspensions and expulsions for all students amounted to 586,280 school days of instruction lost (Woolard, 2017)!

We use Virginia as a microcosm of a nationwide problem of exclusionary discipline. According to the Civil Rights Data Collection (2020), in 2015–2016, of the 50.5 million students enrolled in US public schools, 2,557,072 students were suspended one or more times, totaling 11,392,474 days missed due to out-of-school suspensions. Figure 1.1 compares Virginia with five other states and the US average as a percent of all students suspended one or more times in 2015–2016. Virginia is equal with the US rate of suspensions of 5.3% (Civil Rights Data Collection, 2020).

When this data is broken down by race, Black students are suspended at more than twice the rate nationally and in each of the six states. Figure 1.2 shows Virginia is below the US rate of Black student suspensions of 11.2% (Civil Rights Data Collection, 2020). Black males with disabilities are suspended at more than *three times* the overall rate across the board. Figure 1.3 shows Virginia nearly equal with the national rate of 15.9% (Civil Rights Data Collection, 2020). By the examples of these states and many others, exclusionary discipline is a punitive system administered indiscriminately and *unfairly* across the United States. Research demonstrates exclusionary discipline is racially biased (Cartledge & Kourea, 2008; Gregory & Mosely, 2010; Simmons-Reed & Cartledge, 2014; Skiba et al., 2002; Staats, 2016; Welsh & Little, 2018).

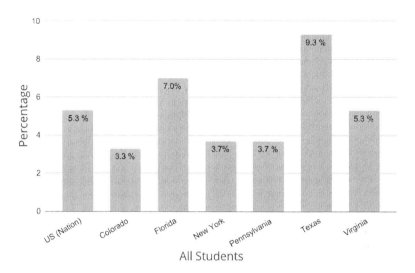

Figure 1.1 Percentage of Students Suspended One or More Times in 2015–2016 (Civil Rights Data Collection, 2020)

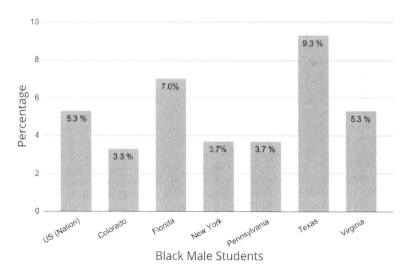

Figure 1.2 Percentage of Black Male Students Suspended in 2015–2016 (Civil Rights Data Collection, 2020)

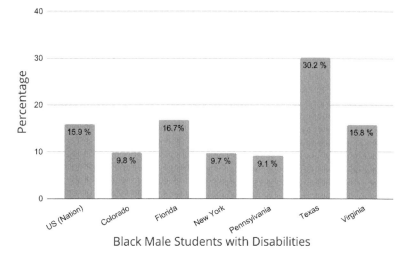

Figure 1.3 Percentage of Black Males with Disabilities Suspended in 2015–2016 (Civil Rights Data Collection, 2020)

Exclusionary Discipline is Racially Biased

The National Education Association (NEA) defines culture as "the everyday experiences, people, events, smells, sounds, and habits of behavior [that shape] a person's sense of who he or she is and where he or she fits in the family, community, and society" (National Education Association, 2018, para. 3). Culture also shapes a student's sense of where he or she fits in the classroom, an identity that a teacher can either alienate or engage. According to Cartledge and Kourea (2008), "Punitive and control measures are the least effective ways to help students become more adaptive in their behavior" (p. 352). By contrast, "Teachers who understand culturally different behaviors respond in ways that appropriately and proactively accept or redirect students' behaviors when necessary" (Cartledge & Kourea, 2008, p. 353). These teachers have cultural competence, "the ability to successfully teach students who come from a culture or cultures other than our own" (National Education Association, 2018, para. 1).

Cultural competence cannot be taught in a single workshop or professional development session. It is a conscious and continuous process of acceptance, respect, and responsiveness that becomes acquired and demonstrated in the policies, structures, practices, attitudes, expectations, and hiring practices of an organization (Substance Abuse and Mental Health Services Administration, 2014). For teachers, cultural competence means valuing and adapting to diversity, being culturally self-aware, understanding the dynamics of difference, and acquiring knowledge of students' culture (National Education Association, 2018). According to researchers at Brown University, culturally responsive teaching is characterized by student-centered instruction that facilitates learning within a positive and relevant context of culture, holds positive perspectives with parents and families, and communicates consistently high expectations for students of every culture (National Education Association, 2018). According to Skiba, Michael, Nardo, and Peterson (2002), "teacher training in appropriate and culturally competent methods of classroom management is likely to be the most pressing need in addressing racial disparities in school discipline" (p. 336).

When lacking cultural competence, teachers or administrators may act on implicit biases that interfere with equitable student instruction and discipline (Staats, 2016). Implicit biases are pervasive, unconscious attitudes or stereotypes that affect our understanding, actions, and decisions (Staats, 2016). All humans have implicit biases, "and they can challenge even the most well-intentioned and egalitarian-minded individuals, resulting in actions and outcomes that do not necessarily align with explicit intentions" (Staats, 2016, p. 29). Implicit biases function on an emotional level as automatic associations of social judgment (Bergland, 2013). Individuals are most likely to rely on these associations in situations that involve ambiguous or incomplete information, time constraints, and fatigue (Staats, 2016). "Given that teachers encounter many, if not all, of these conditions through the course of a school day, it is unsurprising that implicit biases may be contributing to teachers' actions and decisions" (Staats, 2016, p. 30).

According to Dr. Ivory Toldson, CEO and President of Quality Education for Minorities Network:

> There are more than six million teachers in the United States; nearly 80% of public school teachers are White, 9.3% are Black, 7.4% are Hispanic, 2.3% are Asian, and 1.2% are another race. The US has one White female teacher for every 15 students and one Black male teacher for every 534 students. (2018)

Such disparity can create a "diversity gap" in which a large number of students do not relate with their teachers, and vice versa, which "creates conditions for cultural discontinuities" (Skiba et al., 2002, p 101). Cultural discontinuities can include "deficit thinking," wherein White teachers have lower academic expectations for Black students, especially males and students with disabilities (SWD) (Cartledge & Kourea, 2008). These students may internalize their low standing in the classroom and can become academically unmotivated and disruptive (Cartledge & Kourea, 2008). Conversely, Good and Nichols (2001) determined "Black students—especially boys—and to a lesser extent other children who come from low income homes, may find their academic scores improperly lowered because of classroom conduct" (p. 121).

Gregory and Mosely (2010) found that an achievement gap for Black students is correlated with a discipline gap. In other words, many Black students are trapped in a cycle of failure and defiance. Gregory and Weinstein (2008) measured "defiance" as a descriptor in office discipline referrals (ODRs) and found Black students were overrepresented by a small number of White teachers. Surveying students who were most often referred, the authors found these students were more likely to be defiant when they perceived their teacher as untrustworthy. The authors concluded these teachers had reacted to norm-violating versus maladaptive behaviors and suggested the teachers were actually provoking the defiance. Welsh and Little (2018) concluded the same:

> Educational settings that subscribe to societal norms generate backlash from students who are unable or unwilling to act outside of their normative behaviors. Teachers view these behaviors as inappropriate, thus warranting some form of consequence. Likewise, students view these teachers as an untrustworthy authoritarian. The dynamic produces a culture of control that impedes the success of [students]. (p. 766)

A culture of control in the classroom can lead to ODRs. Skiba et al. (2002) observed that ODRs disproportionately affect Black students. In their study, "Black students are more likely to be referred to the office for more subjective reasons" (p. 335). White students were most often referred to the office for more objective code of conduct violations, such as smoking or vandalism, while Black students were most often referred for subjective violations such as disrespect, excessive noise, and threats. Skiba et al. (2002) concluded, "Teachers who are prone to accepting stereotypes of adolescent African-American males as threatening or dangerous may overreact to relatively minor threats to authority, especially if their anxiety is paired with a misunderstanding of cultural norms of social interaction" (p. 336).

Principals may suspend students to support their teachers. Skiba et al. (2002) identified "a robust pattern in which Black students are suspended disproportionately due primarily to a higher rate of office referrals [and] a general over-reliance on negative and punitive discipline" (p. 335). Their study found suspensions functioned "to pass along the racial discrepancies originating at the level of referral to the office" and reflected "a consistent rank ordering in the likelihood of office referral: Black male, White male, Black female, White female" (Skiba et al., 2002, pp. 333–334). Simmons-Reed and Cartledge (2014) found that White students are more often suspended by administrators for non-discretionary offenses, such as weapons or drugs; Black students are more often suspended by administrators for discretionary offenses such as having a cell phone or disrupting class.

Virginia's data reflect these findings. In 2016–2017, the vast majority of all Virginia suspensions were for "the three D's:" Defiance, Disruption, and Disrespect, each a discretionary offense (Woolard, Salas, & Deane, 2018). The suspension rate in 2016–2017 for Black students "was 4.5 times larger than the suspension rate for Hispanic and White students" (Woolard, Salas, & Deane, 2018, p. 6). Figure 1.4 shows that all Virginia suspensions in 2016–2017 followed the rank order of race and gender observed by Skiba et al. (2002), except Black females were the second most suspended. Concurrently, these suspensions affected SWD significantly more and at similar ratios of disproportionality. According to Skiba et al. (2005), "a relationship between racial or ethnic disparities in discipline and special education referral may be further evidence of a general inability on the part of schools to accommodate cultural differences in behavior, particularly for African American students" (p. 141). In this study, "district rate of school suspension and expulsion proved to be the most robust predictor of special education disproportionality" (Skiba et al., 2005, p. 141).

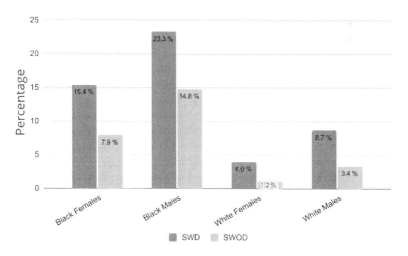

Figure 1.4 Disproportionality of Black Students Suspended in Virginia, 2016–17 (Woolard, Salas, & Deane, 2018)

Bradshaw et al. (2010) found Black teachers also refer a disproportionate number of Black students to the principal's office. A *Harvard Education Review* study of hiring practices in a large unidentified public school district found Black teachers were disproportionately hired in schools with high rates of low-income and minority students (Klein, 2017). According to the Commonwealth Institute for Fiscal Analysis (2017), teachers hired in schools with high rates of low-income and minority students are less experienced. Ferguson (2003) suggested that less experienced teachers need help learning to work with some of the challenges "children from disadvantaged backgrounds may present" (p. 42).

To be certain, Skiba et al. (2005) found no consistent relationship between poverty and disproportionality of special education except that poverty magnifies already existing racial disparities. They further cautioned that "this emphasis on individual socioeconomic disadvantage serves to distract attention from continuing structural inequalities in education that serve to replicate disadvantage in our society" (Sleeter, 1995; Valencia, 1997). Skiba et al. (2005) concluded that a further such structural inequality "may simply be that poorer, predominantly minority districts have fewer resources for handling both learning and behavior problems in the classroom and thus refer more students from the classroom for both discipline and special education service" (Skiba et al., 2005, p. 141). "Discipline philosophy" (e.g., zero-tolerance) also appears to be a systemic variable that contributes to disproportionality (Skiba et al., 2005, p. 142). "To better understand and especially address the causes of [racial] disproportionality, it is critical that efforts continue to be made to identify both the individual and the systemic factors that create and maintain educational inequity" (Skiba et al., 2005, p. 142). Poverty is a profound educational inequity that affects individual school readiness and reduces community resources available to schools (McLoyd, 1998). Other research shows that exclusionary discipline sustains poverty (Center for Community Change, 2020; Loveless, 2017; Soto-Vigil Koon, 2013; U.S. Department of Health and Human Services and U.S. Department of Education, 2014).

Exclusionary Discipline Sustains Poverty

In *Suspended Progress 2018*, Legal Aid Justice Center noted significant concern about what they did not see in Virginia's discipline data.

> What happened to these students after they were suspended or expelled? Where and how did they continue to be educated, and were they still making adequate progress toward graduation? Did they return to their home schools? Were they educated at all? (Woolard, Salas, & Deane, p. 1)

Suspending students to better engage them in school is counterintuitive and counterproductive. After being suspended, students generally "encounter more negative life outcomes than those who are not" (Soto-Vigil Koon, 2013, p. 2). According to the Chief Justice Earl Warren Institute on Law and Social Policy at University of California at Berkeley School of Law, "Children who are suspended miss critical instruction time and often find themselves further behind their peers when they return to school, creating a cycle of lower academic achievement and disengagement from school" (Soto-Vigil Koon, 2013, p. 2). Understandably, behaviors repeat themselves after suspensions when the underlying causes of misbehavior are not addressed and students "have both academic and reputational challenges to overcome" (Woolard, 2017, p. 4). According to the US Department of Health and Human Services (HHS) and US Department of Education (DOE):

> Expulsion or suspension early in a child's education is associated with expulsion or suspension in later school grades…Not only do these practices have the potential to hinder social-emotional and behavioral development, they also remove children from early learning environments and the corresponding cognitively enriching experiences that contribute to healthy development and academic success later in life. (2014, p. 3)

Effectively, exclusionary discipline in preschool and elementary school fosters exclusionary discipline in middle and high school (Evans Cuellar & Markowitz, 2015). According to the US Department of Justice (DOJ) and DOE (2014), a correlation also exists among exclusionary discipline practices and school avoidance, decreased academic achievement, increased behavior problems, increased likelihood of dropping out, substance abuse, and involvement with juvenile justice systems. Students who are expelled or suspended are *10 times* more likely to be incarcerated than their unsuspended peers (HHS & DOE, 2014, p. 3)!

Because suspensions and expulsions disproportionately affect Black students and SWD, the "school-to-prison pipeline" disproportionately affects those same students. According to the American Civil Liberties Union (2020):

> The school-to-prison pipeline is a disturbing national trend wherein children are funneled out of public schools and into the juvenile and criminal justice systems. Many of these children have learning disabilities or histories of poverty, abuse, or neglect, and would benefit from additional educational and counseling services. Instead, they are isolated, punished, and pushed out…"Zero-tolerance" policies criminalize

minor infractions of school rules, while cops in school lead to students being criminalized for behavior that should be handled inside the school. Students of color are especially vulnerable to push-out trends and the discriminatory application of discipline. (para 1–2)

In 2015, Virginia's public schools ranked *first* in the nation by the Center for Public Integrity (CPI) for the number of public school student referrals to law enforcement; CPI analyzed 2011–2012 DOE data and found Virginia schools referred students to police at a rate of 16 for every 1,000 students, *almost triple the national rate*, with the highest rate of referrals in middle schools (Ferris, 2015). At one school more than 200 students were arrested over a five-month period; 77% of those arrested were Black, despite representing only 38% of student enrollment (Ferris, 2015). Police complaints were mostly for "simple assault" or "disorderly conduct," and "almost half of the students issued criminal complaints were children 14 or younger" (Ferris, 2015, para. 36).

Figure 1.5 illustrates the near-identical rate nationally at which people of color are arrested for school-related offenses and incarcerated. According to the Center for Community Change (2020), incarceration contributes to poverty by creating employment barriers, reducing lifetime and intergenerational earnings, removing primary earners and draining assets of low-income families, limiting access to public benefits, and disrupting the social and economic fabric of neighborhoods.

While exclusionary discipline sustains poverty, poverty sustains exclusionary discipline. According to the Brown Center on Education Policy

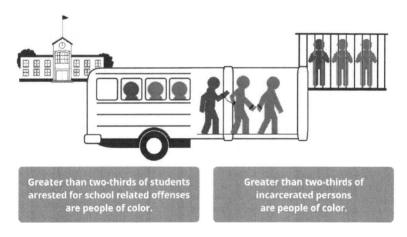

Greater than two-thirds of students arrested for school related offenses are people of color.

Greater than two-thirds of incarcerated persons are people of color.

Figure 1.5 United States School-to-Prison Pipeline (US Department of Education, 2014)

on American Education, "the proportion of high-suspension-rate schools increases in tandem with increased poverty" (Loveless, 2017, para. 20). This correlation is especially apparent in large schools with presumably greater reliance on zero-tolerance discipline policies (Loveless, 2017). The Brown Center also connected high rates of Black student suspensions with high rates of single-parent households. "Children ages 12–17 that come from single-parent families are at least twice as likely to be suspended as children from two-parent families" (Loveless, 2017, para. 25). According to the Annie E. Casey Foundation (Kids Count Data Center, 2020), approximately two-thirds of all Black students in the United States are from single-parent families. The US Census Bureau reports that approximately 39% of US children who are under the age of 18 in single-parent families live under the poverty line (2018).

The top 10 Virginia school divisions cited in *Suspended Progress* for the highest number of short-term suspensions had Black student suspension rates significantly exceeding Black student enrollment percentages (Woolard, 2017). At the same time, Black student suspension rates in these divisions roughly mirrored their free and reduced lunch (poverty) rates (Woolard, 2017; VDOE, 2016). Data showed Virginia divisions with the most suspensions had some of the highest rates of students living in poverty, and a consistent majority of those students suspended were Black. According to Gorski (2018), the median wealth of White households is "13 times greater" than that of Black households (p. 49). "It stands to reason that [Black students] are significantly more likely than [White students] to live in poverty" (Gorski, 2018, p. 49). By extension, they are more likely to be suspended.

Administering student discipline through a deficit-lens of poverty is a likely culprit of this disproportionality. Bomer, Dorwin, May, and Semingson (2008), for example, condemn a blame-the-victim perspective they believe is taken in Dr. Ruby Payne's book, *A Framework for Understanding Poverty* (a text frequently utilized in teacher training). Payne (2005) contends that children in poverty have patterns of thought and social interaction that are unique to poverty and often incompatible with middle-class norms of behavior expected in public schools. While Payne clearly advocates for teaching discipline versus administering discipline, Bomer et al. (2008) criticize the notion that students living in poverty are what must be fixed versus the inequity of poverty itself.

Nowhere in her book does Payne state that poverty, rather than the poor, is the problem that must be addressed. She offers no perspective that people should hold elected officials accountable for the number of families in poverty, or the conditions in which people must live when

their incomes are low…According to such a perspective, neither structural inequality, nor public policy, nor barriers to good jobs, nor lack of
money cause the plight of the poor; they just don't have the right story
structure, or tone of voice, or register, or cognitive strategies. (p. 25–26)

Gorski (2018) prefers to replace the value- and blame-laden term of poverty with *economic marginalization*, "the result of a series of conditions that
deny some people access to resources and opportunities granted to others"
(p. 8). For parents, economic marginalization may include living in food
deserts, working multiple low wage jobs, not having health insurance, not
being able to afford preventive or prenatal care, not having unpaid leave,
not being able to attend school events, not being able to afford child care,
and experiencing school as unwelcome or even hostile due to the false ste-
reotype that economically marginalized parents do not value or want to be
involved in their child's education (Gorski, 2018). For students, economic
marginalization may lead to a life no different than their parents. Without
support structures at home, in their communities, or at school, children from
low-income households can be caught in a trap of generational poverty, or
as Gorski (2018) prefers, *generational injustice*.

Gorski (2018) believes a language distinction must be made between
looking at poverty through a deficit lens (*generational poverty*) versus a
systemic lens (*generational injustice*). The former frames poverty as a personal failure or dysfunctional cultural mindset. The latter identifies it as "a
social condition attached to a long list of inequitable systems and structures,
including public education" (p. 65). Exclusionary discipline is one of those
systems.

Exclusionary Discipline Contributes to Childhood Trauma

While sustaining poverty, exclusionary discipline contributes to childhood
trauma. Hughes (2018) identified a strong relationship between poverty
and exposure to adverse childhood experiences (ACEs) (p. 124). Adverse
childhood experiences may include violence, hunger, parental incarceration, parental abuse and neglect, divorce, and other forms of trauma (Felitti
et al., 1998; Hughes, 2018). According to the Child and Adolescent Health
Measurement Initiative (2017):

ACEs are common across all income groups, though 58% of US
children with ACEs live in homes with incomes less than 200% of
the federal poverty level. ACEs are common across all race/ethnic-
ity groups, though are somewhat disproportionately lower for White
and Non-Hispanic, and lowest for Asian children. Black children are

disproportionately represented among children with ACEs. Over 6 in 10 have ACEs, representing 17.4% of all children in the US with ACEs. (para. 3)

Children who live in urban communities with high poverty rates have a greater likelihood of frequent and intense exposure to trauma, risk for future victimization, and perpetration of violence (Hughes, 2018). Such cumulative exposure to adversity causes stress that behaves as a toxin in the developing brain of a child (Hughes, 2018, p. 124). According to the American Public Health Association (2018):

Chronic stress is a response to persistent social, physical and emotional pressures over an extended period of time. Individuals who experience chronic stress are likely to have consistently high levels of cortisol, the body's primary stress-inducing hormone...If left untreated, chronic stress can contribute to fear, anxiety, depression, attention and concentration problems, an increase in impulsive or risk-taking behavior and– particularly among boys–hostility, aggression and violence. (p. 3)

Evans and Kim (2013) discovered children from low income homes are not only more prone to chronic stress than their peers in higher-income homes but also have "multiple self-regulatory deficits" as a result (p. 45). "Their parents and teachers rate them as less competent in self-control, they have more trouble delaying gratification, they manifest attentional-control problems, they exhibit weaker inhibitory control, and they have diminished capacity for working memory" (Evans & Kim, 2013, p. 45). Furthermore, they acquire limited coping skills from impoverished social environments (Evans & Kim, 2013). For example, children from low-income homes may have stressful social interactions with parents or siblings who are also suffering from chronic stress. They may also find minimal positive reinforcement to adapt productively at childcare, in the neighborhood, or at school (Evans & Kim, 2013).

School can be another traumatic experience when students face exclusionary discipline. Steinberg and Lacoe (2017) reported that 92% of 500 superintendents surveyed in 2014 believe school suspensions are associated with negative student outcomes, including lost instructional time, student disengagement, absenteeism, truancy, and dropout rates. In some instances, a student may experience re-traumatization when serving an OSS (Santiago, Raviv, & Jaycox, 2018). For example, a student who is left at home alone with very little food to eat may experience compounded trauma as a result of being suspended and sent home for a specified number of school days. According to the American Public Health Association (2018), chronic stress is linked to student disengagement and absenteeism. "The cycle of stress is continually perpetuated as motivation decreases and stress-induced behaviors are misunderstood, punished and stigmatized" (p. 5).

In the original 1998 ACEs study conducted by Fellitti et al., subjects were largely White, college-educated adults who reported their exposure to ten events: "emotional, physical, or sexual abuse; physical or emotional neglect; witnessing domestic violence; parental separation or divorce; and living with household members who were substance abusers, mentally ill or suicidal, or ever imprisoned" (Persyn, 2016, p. 3). Of the ten, 12.5% reported having experienced four or more ACEs. In 2012, the Institute for Safe Families (ISF) conducted a study of ACEs experienced in an urban population. The ISF survey studied a sample of urban Philadelphia residents who were 44% White, 43% Black, 42% with a high school education (or some high school).

> The survey found that 33.2% of Philadelphia adults experienced emotional abuse and 35% experienced physical abuse during childhood; about 35% grew up in a house with a substance-abusing member; 24% lived with a person who was mentally ill; and 13% counted an incarcerated person among their household. Overall, 68% experienced at least one of the original ACEs. (Persyn, 2016, p. 4)

In addition, the Philadelphia ACE Task Force developed an urban ACE module. Urban ACE Indicators included the original ACEs plus experiencing racism, witnessing violence, living in an unsafe neighborhood, living in foster care, and enduring bullying. Behaviors and health outcomes included "multiple sexual partners, smoking, suicide attempt, substance abuse, cancer, diabetes, obesity, asthma, and mental illness" (Persyn, 2016, p. 4).

> The results were striking. Nearly 41% of the survey respondents had witnessed violence while growing up; 35% experienced discrimination based on race or ethnicity; 27% reported feeling unsafe in their neighborhoods during childhood. Overall, 58% experienced at least one of the five Urban Indicators; 81% experienced at least one of the 14 total ACEs; and 45% experienced at least one of the original ACEs and at least one Urban Indicator. (Persyn, 2016, p. 4)

According to Persyn (2016) the Philadelphia data "appear to show a strong correlation between race, poverty, and levels of ACEs exposure that are high enough to pose very significant threats to the physical and mental health of affected residents" (p. 18). Persyn further cites US Census data that reveals an intersection with race. She found, "of the six zip codes with the highest ACE scores, four have a population at least 50% African

American and two are 80% African American and over" (Persyn, 2016, p. 18). Persyn (2016) concludes, "The burden of ACEs is born, in large part, by those children least able to access the resources and support structures that could help them build resilience to traumatic experiences" (p. 20).

Resilience is the Key to Reform

Resilience is "the process of adapting well in the face of adversity, trauma, tragedy, threats or significant sources of stress" (American Psychological Association, 2012, para. 4). According to Persyn (2016), school can be an opportunity to build resilience for all children.

> As our understanding of child trauma and toxic stress crystallizes, schools have a unique opportunity to view student conduct through a trauma lens and consider whether neurobiological and physiological responses to toxic stress have an undue influence over students' actions. The purpose is not to disregard the conduct, nor to avoid confronting problems of bias in school discipline, but rather to make use of the conduct as a red flag for psychological and physiological distress. Through the use of restorative justice and other innovative techniques, school staff can ask not "what is wrong with you?" but rather "what happened to you?" These questions are of particularly acute importance to poor students of color, who, due to this intersection of identities, carry the heaviest burden of stress. Easing that physiological and emotional burden will go far to support these students and promote their success. (p. 22)

Evans and Kim (2013) found that children from low-income homes with better self-regulatory and coping skills are more resilient to traumatic experiences. In turn, they are more engaged in school academically, socially, and emotionally. With adult support and instruction, and through trauma-informed discipline practices, schools can systematically help students to develop resilience. Developing resilience is restorative versus punitive, equitable versus discriminating, empowering versus impoverishing, and trauma-responsive versus trauma-producing. Developing resilience in all children is the key to solving the problems of exclusionary discipline.

References

American Civil Liberties Union. (2020). School-to-prison pipeline. Retrieved from https://www.aclu.org/issues/juvenile-justice/school-prison-pipeline/school-priso n-pipeline?redirect=feature/school-prison-pipeline.

American Public Health Association. (2018, March). *Chronic stress and the risk of high school dropout* (Issue Brief, March 1, 2018). Washington, DC.

American Psychological Association. (2012). Building your resilience. Retrieved from https://www.apa.org/topics/resilience.

Bergland, C. (2013, January 22). Cortisol: Why the "stress hormone" is public enemy no. 1. *Psychology Today*. Retrieved from https://www.psychologytod ay.com/us/blog/the-athletes-way/201301/cortisol-why-the-stress-hormone -is- public-enemy-no-1.

Bomer, R., Dworin, J. E., May, L., & Semingson, P. (2008). Miseducating teachers about the poor: A critical analysis of Ruby Payne's claims about poverty. *Teachers College Record, 110*(12), 2497–2531. Retrieved from http://sites.nd .edu/poverty-cap/files/2012/07/TCRecord_Payne_Critique.pdf.

Bradshaw, C. P., Mitchell, M. M., O'Brennan, L. M., & Leaf, P. J. (2010). Multilevel exploration of factors contributing to the overrepresentation of black students in office disciplinary referrals. *Journal of Educational Psychology, 102*(2), 508–520. doi: doi.org/10.1037/a0018450.

Cartledge, G., & Kourea, L. (2008). Culturally responsive classrooms for culturally diverse students with and at risk for disabilities. *Exceptional Children, 74*(3), 351–371. doi: 10.1177/001440290807400305.

Center for Community Change. (2020). The relationship between poverty and mass incarceration: How mass incarceration contributes to poverty in the United States. Retrieved from https://www.masslegalservices.org/system/files/library/ The_Relationship_between_Poverty_and_Mass_Incarceration.pdf.

Civil Rights Data Collection. (2020). *School/district/state comparison report.* [Data set]. Retrieved from https://ocrdata.ed.gov/DataAnalysisTools/DataSetBuilder ?Report=1.

The Commonwealth Institute for Fiscal Analysis. (2017, October). *Unequal opportunities: Fewer resources, worse outcomes for students in schools with concentrated poverty* (Issue Brief, October, 26, 2017). Richmond, VA: Chris Duncombe.

Evans, G. W., & Kim, P. (2013, March). Childhood poverty, chronic stress, self-regulation, and coping. *Childhood Development Perspectives, 7*(1). 43–48. doi: 10.1111/cdep.12013.

Evans Cuellar, A., & Markowitz, S. (2015, August). School suspension and the school-to-prison pipeline. *International Review of Law and Economics, 43*, 98–106. doi: 10.1016/j.irle.2015.06.001.

Exclusionary Discipline. (2018). National clearinghouse on supportive school discipline. Retrieved from https://supportiveschooldiscipline.org/learn/refer ence-guides/exclusionary-discipline.

Felitti, V., Anda, R., Nordenberg, D., Williamson, D., Spitz, A., Edwards, V., … Marks, J. (1998). Relationship to childhood abuse and household dysfunction to many of the leading causes of death in adults: The adverse childhood experiences (ACE) study. *American Journal of Preventive Medicine, 14*(4), 245–258. doi: 10.1016/S0749-3797(98)00017-8.

Ferguson, R. F. (2003). Teachers' perceptions and expectations and the black-white test score gap. *Urban Education, 38*(4). 460–507. doi: 10.1177/0042085903038004006.

Ferris, S. (2015, April 10). Virginia tops nation in sending students to cops, courts: Where does your state rank? Center for Public Integrity. Retrieved from https ://www.publicintegrity.org/2015/04/10/17089/virginia-tops-nation-sending-st udents-cops-courts-where-does-your-state-rank.

Good, T. L., & Nichols, S. L. (2001) Expectancy effects in the classroom: A special focus on improving the reading performance of minority students in first-grade classrooms. *Educational Psychologist, 36*(2), 113–126. doi: 10.1207/ S15326985EP3602_6\.

Gorski, P. C. (2018). *Reaching and teaching students in poverty: Strategies for erasing the opportunity gap,* 2nd ed. New York: Teachers' College Press.

Gregory, A., & Mosely, P. M. (2010). The discipline gap: Teachers' views on the over-representation of African American students in the discipline system. *Equity & Excellence in Education, 37*(1), 18–30. doi: 10.1080/10665680490429280.

Gregory, A., & Weinstein, R. S. (2008). The discipline gap and African Americans: Defiance or cooperation in the high school classroom. *Journal of School Psychology, 46*(4), 455–475. doi: 10.1016/j.jsp.2007.09.001.

Hughes, M. (2018). Poverty as an adverse childhood experience. *North Carolina Medical Journal, 79*(2), 124–126. doi: 10.18043/ncm.79.2.124.

Kids Count Data Center. (2020). *Children in single-parent families by race in the United States.* The Annie E. Casey Foundation. Retrieved from https://datacenter .kidscount.org/data/tables/107-children-in-single-parent-families-by#detailed/1/ any/false/573,869,36,868,867/10,11,9,12,1,185,13/432,431.

Klein, R. (2017, April 14). Why aren't there more black teachers? Racial discrimination still plays a role. *Huffington Post.* Retrieved from https:// www.huffingtonpost.com/entry/teacher-racism-black-discrimination_us _58ebdcc2e4b0c89f912083dc.

Langberg, J., & Ciolfi, A. (2016). Suspended progress (Research Report May 2016). Retrieved from https://www.justice4all.org/wp-content/uploads/2016/05/Suspe nded-Progress-Report.pdf.

Lhamon, C. E., Timmons-Goodson, P., Abegbile, D. P., Herriot, G. L., Kirsanow, P. N., Kladney, D., Narasaki, K., & Yaki, M. (2019, July). *Beyond suspensions: Examining school discipline policies and connections to the school-to-prison pipeline for students of color with disabilities.* The United States Commission on Civil Rights. Retrieved from https://www.usccr.gov/pubs/2019/07-23-Beyond-Suspensions.pdf.

Loveless, T. (2017). *How well are American students learning?* Houston, TX: Brown Foundation, Inc. Retrieved from https://www.brookings.edu/wp-content/ uploads/2017/03/2017-brown-center-report-on-american-education.pdf.

McLoyd, V. C. (1998). Socioeconomic disadvantage and child development. *American Psychologist, 53*(2), 185–204. https://doi.org/10.1037/0003-066X.53 .2.185

National Child Traumatic Stress Network, Schools Committee. (2017). *Creating, supporting, and sustaining trauma-informed schools: A system framework.* Los Angeles, CA: National Center for Child Traumatic Stress.

National Education Association. (2018). Why cultural competence? To help educators close achievement gaps. Retrieved from http://www.nea.org/home /39783.htm.

Payne, R. (2005). *A framework for understanding poverty*, 4th ed. Highlands, TX: Aha! Process, Inc.

Persyn, M. K. (2016). *Agents of progress: Schools and child traumatic stress.* Poverty & Race Research Action Council. Retrieved from Ethnic NewsWatch Retrieved from http://proxy.library.vcu.edu/login?url=https://searchhttp://-pr oquest-com.proxy.library.vcu.edu/docview/1861256926?accountid=14780.

Santiago, C., Raviv, T., & Jaycox, L. (2018). *Universal and schoolwide interventions for trauma* (p. 37–52). Washington, DC: American Psychological Association.

Simmons-Reed, E. A., & Cartledge, G. (2014). School discipline disproportionality: Culturally competent interventions for African American males. *Interdisciplinary Journal of Teaching and Learning, 4*(2), 95–109. doi: 10.1177/001440290807400305.

Skiba, R. J., Michael, R. S., Nardo, A. C., & Peterson, R. (2002). The color of discipline: Sources of racial and gender disproportionality in school punishment. *The Urban Review, 34*(4), 317–342. doi: 10.1023/A:1021320817372.

Skiba, R. J., Poloni-Staudinger, L., Simmons, A. B., Feggins-Azziz, L. R., & Chung, C. (2005). Unproven links: Can poverty explain ethnic disproportionality in special education. *The Journal of Special Education, 39*(3), 130–144. Retrieved from https://files.eric.ed.gov/fulltext/EJ722287.pdf.

Sleeter, C. E. (1995). Foreword. In B. B. Swadener & S. Lubeck (Eds.), *Children and families 'at Promise': Deconstructing the discourse of risk.* Albany, NY: State University of New York Press.

Soto-Vigil Koon, D. (2013). Exclusionary discipline: An issue brief and review of the literature. *The Chief Justice Earl Warren Institute on Law and Social Policy, 39*(1), 317–342. doi: 10.3102/001389X09357621.

Staats, C. (2016). Understanding implicit bias: What educators should know. *American Educator, 39*(4), 29–34. Retrieved from https://files.eric.ed.gov/full text/EJ1086492.pdf.

Steinberg, M., & Lacoe, J. (2017). What do we know about school discipline reform? Assessing the alternatives to suspensions and expulsions. *Education Next, 17*(1), 44–52.

Substance Abuse and Mental Health Services Administration. (2014). *Guiding principles of trauma-informed care. 22*(2). Retrieved from https://www.samhsa .gov/samhsaNewsLetter/Volume_22_Number_2/trauma_tip/guiding_principles .html.

Toldson, I. (2018, July 24). Deconstructing the achievement gap to move from equity to excellence. In L. Walker (Chair), *Virginia is for all learners: Education equity summer institute.* Symposium conducted at the meeting of the Virginia Department of Education in Richmond, VA.

US Census Bureau. (2018). Poverty rate and percentage point change by type of family: Families and people. Retrieved from https://www.census.gov/content/ dam/Census/library/visualizations/2019/demo/p60-266/Figure9.pdf.

US Department of Health and Human Services, U.S. Department of Education. (2014). Policy statement on expulsion and suspension policies in early childhood settings (HHS Publication No. 187050). Retrieved from http://www.docslides .com/danika-pritchard/u-s-department-of-health-and-human-servicesu-s-depart ment.

US Department of Justice, US Department of Education. (2014). Dear colleague letter: Nondiscriminatory administration of school discipline (January 8, 2014). Retrieved from https://www2.ed.gov/about/offices/list/ocr/letters/colleague -201401-title-vi.html.

Valencia, R. R. (1997). *The evolution of deficit thinking: Educational thought and practice*. London: Falmer Press.

Virginia Department of Education Office of Nutrition Programs. (2016). School year 2015–2016 National School Lunch Program (NSLP) free and reduced price eligibility report: Division level. Retrieved from http://www.doe.virginia.gov/. support/nutrition/statistics/free_reduced_eligibility/2015-2016/divisions/frpe_d iv_report_sy2015-16.pdf.

Welsh, R. O., & Little, S. (2018, October). The school discipline dilemma: A comprehensive review of disparities and alternative approaches. *Review of Educational Research, 88*(5), 752–794. doi: 10.3102/0034654318791582.

Woolard, A. (2017). Suspended progress 2017: An update on the state of exclusionary discipline in Virginia's public schools (Research Reports October 2017). Retrieved From https://www.justice4all.org/wp-content/uploads/2016 /04/Suspended-Progress-2017.pdf.

Woolard, A., Salas, M., & Deane, R. (2018). Suspended progress, 2018: An update on the state of exclusionary discipline and alternative education in Virginia's public schools (Research Report October 2018). Retrieved from https://www.jus tice4all.org/wpcontent/uploads/2018/10/FullSuspendedProgress2018.pdf.

2 Looking Through the Lenses of Trauma and Resilience

We have established that exclusionary discipline fails to improve social and academic outcomes for children with ACEs and trauma. It may further subject children to additional trauma. According to the Legal Aid Justice Center:

> [Schools'] use of exclusionary discipline is myopic and harmful. Suspensions and expulsions place students out of sight and out of mind, but they don't disappear. These are often children who—still forming as people—need academic, social, and therapeutic supports, and positive adult guidance, more than ever. When students are struggling, they need more help, not less. When students become disconnected from their education, they need more support, not less. When students are misbehaving, they need more attention from the adults in their lives, not less.
>
> (Woolard, 2017, p. 5)

Understanding the impact of ACEs and trauma on brain development and behavior is a critical first step to providing children who are struggling with more help, support, and attention from the adults in their lives. At the same time, understanding that the brain can rewire itself through trauma-responsive practices is critical to avoid deficit-thinking and embrace the power of resilience. In this chapter, we provide an overview of the brain science of ACEs and trauma, identify the effects of ACEs and trauma on child behavior and the physical and mental health of adults, explore the brain's power of resilience, and make the case for trauma-responsive discipline.

The Brain Science of ACEs and Trauma

Adverse childhood experiences have significant impacts on brain development. "Brain development is directed by genes but sculpted by experiences, particularly those occurring during early sensitive or critical periods" (Teicher et al., 2016, p. 652). Adverse childhood experiences often have "long-lasting effects on brain function, cognitive and emotional development, and can influence the risk to develop stress related psychopathology later in life" (Krugers et al., 2017, p. 15). Adverse childhood experiences can change the amount of gray matter and the integrity of white matter in the brain, which can negatively affect processing of information and communication between areas of the brain.

Krugers et al. (2017) determined that ACEs result in decreased higher cognitive functions, contextual memory, and executive function due to reduced volumes of the hippocampus and prefrontal cortex. Conversely, there is an increase in the activation of the amygdala, which causes difficulty with emotional learning and expressions of fear. Adverse childhood experiences affect multiple areas of the brain including the hippocampus, prefrontal cortex, amygdala, corpus callosum, hypothalamus, and occipital lobe.

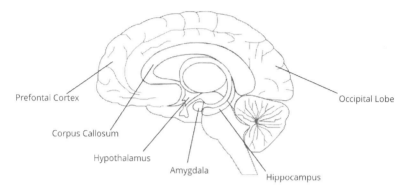

Figure 2.1 Areas of the Brain Affected by ACEs

Area of the Brain	Function	Impact of ACEs	Additional Information
Hippocampus	Critical for learning, memory, and regulating emotion	Decreased volume	Activated by stress
Frontal Cortex	Decision making and social/emotional regulation	Decreased volume	Damaged by emotional maltreatment and sexual abuse
Amygdala	Fight, flight, or freeze responses Perception of reward	Increased volume	Especially sensitive between the ages of 9 and 13
Corpus Callosum	Physical coordination and complex processing	Reduced volume and integrity	Twice as much loss in males exposed to maltreatment as females
Hypothalamus	Activates the adrenal gland to release stress hormones related to anxiety and fear	Increased production of stress hormones	Activated by stress
Occipital Lobe	Visual memory and processing	Reduced gray matter density and thickness	Most impacted by domestic violence and sexual abuse

Figure 2.2 Potential Impact of ACEs on Areas of the Brain (Heim & Binder, 2012; Krugers et al., 2017; McClelland et al., 2011; Teicher et al., 2016)

Hippocampus

The hippocampus, located near the center of the brain, is critical for learning and memory, and is activated by stress. McClelland et al. (2011) determined that enriched early life experiences improve hippocampal-dependent learning and memory. However, because of the high number of hormone receptors, the hippocampus is unusually vulnerable to stress and is significantly affected by ACEs (McClelland et al., 2011). The stress hormone exposure decreases the volume of the hippocampus by causing early cell death, decreased cell formation, and progressive loss of dendritic arbors and spines (Bath, Manzano-Nieves, & Goodwill, 2016). Heim and Binder (2012) found that individuals with ACEs typically have a smaller hippocampus, especially if the trauma involved sexual abuse between the ages of three and five, and between 11 and 13 (sexual abuse can impact other parts of the brain at other ages). McClelland et al. (2011) similarly found a smaller hippocampal volume in individuals who have experienced chronic childhood stress, leading to impairments which are potentially progressive in the hippocampal structure and function. Childhood poverty has also been shown to impact the volume of the hippocampus; however, caregiver support can limit this impact (Krugers et al., 2017). Additionally, maternal care has a strong impact on the development of the hippocampus and its synaptic plasticity (Lutz & Turecki, 2014). Maternal deprivation increases levels of stress hormones, resulting in memory deficits and despair (Lutz & Turecki, 2014).

Prefrontal Cortex

The prefrontal cortex is located at the front of the brain and is important for decision making and social-emotional regulation. According to Heim and Binder (2012), emotional maltreatment can decrease the volume of the frontal cortex. Decreases in volume of the prefrontal cortex are associated with difficulties in social and emotional regulatory behavior and are most commonly found in women who experienced sexual abuse between the ages of 14 and 16 (Heim & Binder, 2012, p. 104). The decreased volume of the prefrontal cortex can also cause a reduction in executive functioning skills, such as organization and decision-making (Krugers et al., 2017).

Amygdala

The amygdala is located near the hippocampus and helps us determine relative danger versus safety, and fight, flight, or freeze responses (Fareri

& Tottenham, 2016). The amygdala is involved in our reactions to events that may impact our survival and our perception of the potential for reward (Fareri & Tottenham, 2016). "Increases in amygdala volumes were linked with difficulties in social and emotional regulatory behavior" (Heim & Binder, 2012, p. 104). Teicher et al. (2016) noted an increased amygdala response to facial expressions, especially when the faces appear threatening (p. 655). Maltreatment is related to a reduction in the gray matter volume of the amygdala and to the integrity and pathways involved in the conscious perception of threat and contextual memories (Teicher et al., 2016, p. 655). Andersen (2016) found elevated amygdala activity in adolescents resulting in a hyper-responsivity to emotional faces (p. 331). For example, a student may interpret a teacher's neutral facial expression as threatening or angry when that is not what the teacher intends to communicate.

Childhood is a time of learning to navigate the world. The ability to understand the environment and how to interact relies heavily on the amygdala and ventral striatum. A great deal of this development depends on caregiver attention and availability. The most rapid rates of change in the amygdala occur prior to adolescence, especially between the ages of nine and 13. During this time period, impacts on the amygdala significantly impact the ability to adapt and function in a social environment (Fareri & Tottenham, 2016).

Corpus Callosum

The corpus callosum is the band of nerves connecting the two sides of the brain. This allows the left and right hemispheres to communicate and control physical coordination and processing of complex information. The corpus callosum is fully developed by the age of 12. Teicher et al. (2016) found individuals who were maltreated had reduced volume and integrity of the corpus callosum. In males, there was twice as much loss as in females, especially when maltreatment occurred. In females, the loss was more significant after sexual abuse (Teicher et al., 2016, p. 659).

Hypothalamus

The hypothalamus is located in the center of the brain and is activated by stress. The hypothalamus activates the adrenal gland to produce stress hormones. The brain is physically impacted by stress hormones, such as cortisol, and their mediators which are released during times of excessive stress and trauma (Bolton et al., 2017; Heim & Binder, 2012). Heim and Binder (2012) identified a connection to stress hormone resistance in the brain. Cortisol, released in response to fear, is related to fight, flight, or freeze responses. An excessive amount of cortisol "interferes with learning and memory, lowers immune function and bone density, increases weight gain, blood pressure, cholesterol, and heart disease" (Bergland, 2013, para. 1). Additionally, the altered expression of hormones and their mediators are related to anxiety and fear in the amygdala, which communicates with the brain regions related to learning, addiction, pleasure, and reward (Bolton et al., 2017).

Occipital Lobe

The lingual gyrus lies on the occipital lobe and is involved in the processing of vision. Individuals who have witnessed domestic violence have a reduction in gray matter density and reduced thickness of other portions of the visual cortex. The most dramatic impact in the reduction of density and thickness occurs when domestic violence is witnessed between the ages of 11 and 13 (Teicher et al., 2016, p. 654).

Sexual abuse, especially before the age of 12, has also been found to be related to a reduction in gray matter in the primary visual cortex and visual association cortices. Decreased visual memory and facial recognition and processing appear to be directly related to the duration of exposure to sexual abuse before the age of 12 (Teicher et al., 2016, p. 655).

The Effects of ACEs and Trauma on Child Behavior

Exposure to ACEs can inhibit functioning of certain areas of the brain which negatively affect a student's ability to make decisions, regulate social and emotional reactions, perceive danger or threats, control physical coordination, process complex information, remember information presented visually, and interpret facial expressions. The heightened presence of stress hormones in the brain inhibit students' ability to access the thinking part of their brain forcing them into fight, flight, or freeze responses. Sporleder states, "Severe and chronic trauma (such as living with an alcoholic parent or watching in terror as your mom gets beat up) causes toxic stress in kids. Toxic stress damages kids' brains" (Stevens, 2012, para. 21).

The timing of ACEs plays a critical role in the impact of trauma (Burns et al., 2018). Seghete et al. (2018) determined the younger the individual, the more activation across a large number of brain areas. The frontal regions, which mature prior to the age of 13, may be permanently affected, leading to a greater reliance on in-the-moment reactions, even in conditions that do not typically involve emotions. Additionally, Seghete et al. (2018) found less activation in the left brain stem and temporal lobe with a younger age of exposure to trauma. They further discovered that early exposure to trauma led to more reactive aspects of cognitive control (Seghete et al., 2018). Andersen (2016) adds early exposure to trauma may cause accelerated development of reactive responses, "serving as an adaptive function to survive in a malevolent world" (p. 330). According to Sporleder, "When trauma launches kids into flight, fight or freeze mode, they cannot learn. It is physiologically impossible" (Stevens, 2012, para. 21).

Children who experience ACEs may demonstrate difficulty regulating their behaviors and emotions due to trauma. Brown et al. (2016) studied the prevalence of ACEs in children with and without diagnosis of moderate to severe Attention Deficit Hyperactivity Disorder (ADHD). The study revealed that children with ACE scores of two or higher "were significantly more likely to have parent-rated moderate to severe ADHD" (Brown et al., 2016, p. 351). These results led researchers to suggest that further studies need to be conducted to determine if "ACE exposure might cause, potentiate, or be misdiagnosed as ADHD, or by which ADHD might be associated with ACEs" (Brown et al., 2016, p. 353).

Cook et al. (2005) identified "seven primary domains of impairment observed in children exposed to trauma: attachment, biology, affect regulation, dissociation (i.e., alterations in consciousness), behavioral regulation, cognition, and self-concept" (p. 392). Briere and Elliott (1994) identified immediate symptoms of trauma to include "frequent re-experiencing of the trauma through nightmares or thoughts," difficulty sleeping, avoidance, and "jumpiness or hyperarousal" (p. 56). Greeson et al. (2011) added "behavioral and emotional reactions, [including] high risk behaviors" (p. 94). Additionally, Cook et al. (2005) included erratic behavior, aggressiveness, extreme responses to minor issues, "extreme helplessness, confusion, withdrawal, or rage" as common reactions for children affected by trauma (p. 392). Childhood trauma often leads to fear and anxiety because it interferes with a "child's developing sense of security and belief in a safe, just world" (Briere & Elliott, 1994, p. 57). Because trauma often happens when children are "physically or psychologically unable to resist or defend" themselves from the sources of trauma, children often believe they caused or deserved what happened to them due to being "inherently bad" (Briere & Elliott, 1994, pp. 56–57).

Anger is a common reaction to childhood trauma and is often expressed as aggression and behavioral problems, such as "fighting, bullying, or attacking other children [which may lead to] increased social isolation and unpopularity" (Briere & Elliott, 1994, p. 58). Additionally, Briere and Elliott (1994) identified "distrust of others, anger at and/or fear of those with greater power, concerns about abandonment, [and] perceptions of injustice" as common responses to childhood trauma (p. 58). "Severe child maltreatment…may interfere with the child's development of a sense of self" (Briere & Elliott, 1994, p. 60). This may lead to avoidance (including spacing-out or daydreaming), substance abuse, suicide, or tension-reducing activities (including binging and purging, chronic overeating, or self-mutilation) (Briere & Elliott, 1994).

The Effects of ACEs and Trauma on the Physical and Mental Health of Adults

Approximately one-third of the US population has experienced some form of ACE (Andersen, 2016). More than 60% of the world's population has experienced at least one ACE and 38% has experienced at least two (Burns et al., 2018). According to Heim and Binder (2012), the National Child Abuse and Neglect Data System received 3,300,000 referrals for 6,000,000 children who were allegedly maltreated in 2009 (the most recent data available). Sixty-one percent of those children received some sort of professional response. However, they believe most cases of maltreatment remain unreported. In 2020, the World Health Organization (WHO) estimated that up to one billion children below the age of 18, "have experienced physical, sexual, or emotional violence or neglect in the past year" (para. 1).

Childhood and adolescence are critical periods of active brain growth. If significant events occur, either positive or negative, the individual may demonstrate a permanent predisposition to a set of behaviors. During these times of active brain growth, the brain is especially sensitive to environmental impacts. This sensitivity is increased during adolescence (Andersen, 2016). According to Anderson (2016), children exposed to ACEs tend to have a nine-year delay in the manifestation of behaviors related to trauma. Behaviors in adolescents may actually stem from trauma in early childhood.

Adverse childhood experiences create alterations to emotional and cognitive brain processes that are often observable into adulthood (Seghete et al., 2018). The impacts of childhood ACEs and trauma on the brain show a relationship to later addictions and the abilities to experience pleasure and control stress (Bolton et al., 2017; McClelland et al., 2011). Heim and Binder (2012) found a strong relationship between trauma and mental health issues into adulthood, including increased risk of anxiety, addiction, and psychiatric admissions. Adults who reported multiple ACEs exhibited a four-fold increase in depression and two to five times the risk of suicide. It is estimated that 67% of suicide attempts and 64% of addiction to drugs cases in the US are related to ACEs. Eliminating ACEs could potentially reduce disorders related to mood, behavior, and substance abuse by almost 30% worldwide (Burns et al., 2018; Teicher et al., 2016).

Bolton et al. (2017) also found a strong association between ACEs and adult depression, alcohol use, and addiction. Additionally, Bolton et al.

(2017) describe a relationship between ACEs and nerve connections related to pleasure and reward resulting in a loss of ability to experience pleasure. According to Felitti et al. (1998), ACEs have a strong relationship to some of the "leading causes of death in adults…including ischemic heart disease, cancer, chronic lung disease, skeletal fractures, and liver disease" (p. 251). Teicher et al. (2016) claim six or more ACEs may result in a 20-year reduction in life span (p. 672).

Fortunately, such accumulation of stress on physical and psychological health is not deterministic. The brain's power of resilience can be healing, sustaining, and life prolonging.

The Brain's Power of Resilience

Not all individuals are affected adversely by ACEs. Stress exposure and ACEs can have contradictory effects on adult outcomes, and in some cases can even be associated with increased resilience to future adversity (Burns et al., 2018, p. 116). Some individuals may actually develop resilience as a result of ACEs (Andersen, 2016; Zannas & West, 2014). Resilience is not a character trait (e.g., *resiliency*), but a dynamic process derived from learning and adapting to survive within the context of adversity (Luthar, Cicchetti, & Becker, 2000). Ginsburg (2018) identifies what behaviors educators should strive to develop in children (see Figure 2.3).

Developing resilience is as much biological as sociological. The brain learns responses to what is "safe" or "dangerous," and continuously "encodes that learning into its neural circuitry" (Graham, 2013, p. 4). According to Graham (2013), such encoding develops through *secure attachment*, *conditioning*, and *neuroplasticity*.

1. **Competence.** When we notice what young people are doing right and give them opportunities to develop important skills, they feel competent. We undermine competence when we don't allow young people to recover themselves after a fall.

2. **Confidence.** Young people need confidence to be able to navigate the world, think outside the box, and recover from challenges.

3. **Connection.** Connections with other people, schools, and communities offer young people the security that allows them to stand on their own and develop creative solutions.

4. **Character.** Young people need a clear sense of right and wrong and a commitment to integrity.

5. **Contribution.** Young people who contribute to the well-being of others will receive gratitude rather than condemnation. They will learn that contributing feels good and may therefore more easily turn to others and do so without shame.

6. **Coping.** Young people who possess a variety of healthy coping strategies will be less likely to turn to dangerous quick fixes when stressed.

7. **Control.** Young people who understand privileges and respect are earned through demonstrated responsibility will learn to make wise choices and feel a sense of control.

Figure 2.3 Ginsburg's Seven Cs of Resilience (Ginsburg, 2018)

Secure Attachment

Evolutionary psychologists believe resilience develops interpersonally. Resilience begins most fundamentally with *secure attachment* to a loving parent or caregiver in infancy and early childhood. If a baby's diaper is changed when she cries, she learns "that calls for help are answered and that solutions to problems exist" (Graham, 2013, p.7). Similarly, "if a growing child sees that his efforts to communicate with a parent are valued and understood, even if the parent can't do what the child wants right then or ever, the child's neural circuits stabilize around a trustworthy sense of his own competence and mastery" (p. 7). However, secure attachment does not have to be from a parent. When viewed ecologically, it can come from an extended family member, teacher, coach, or school counselor and last into adulthood. Secure attachment reduces risk factors, such as poverty, and increases with protective factors, such as health care, safety, nutrition, and coping skills. The strongest protective factor of all is the reliable presence of a nurturing and responsive adult who provides unconditional love, high expectations, and modeling of positive coping behaviors (Bartlett, Smith, & Bringewatt, 2017; National Scientific Council on the Developing Child, 2014; Ginsburg & Jablow, 2020). The more a child learns and expects that fear and anxiety will be comforted by a trusted caregiver, the memory of that comfort can buffer the child with stable coping strategies to stress or other trauma later in life (Graham, 2013). Neuroscientists call this process *conditioning*.

Conditioning

Over time, conditioning results in an automatic response to stimuli. According to Graham (2013), "No matter what the external trigger, it's our internal response, based on our neural wiring, that is important for resilience" (p. 12). In other words, when faced with stress or trauma, our learned responses take over. Neural wiring can develop from and contribute to negative coping patterns that are reactive and self-defeating, making individuals ever more vulnerable to stress and trauma. Negative coping patterns can also be detrimental to learning and positive neural development. On the other hand, new conditioning, deconditioning, and reconditioning are ways "to rewire previous patterns of response that are less resilient, or even dysfunctional" (p. 13). Although our brains are wired early in life, "we know that later experiences, especially healthy relational ones, can undo or overwrite that early learning to help us cope differently and more resiliently with anything, anything at all" (p. 5).

Neuroplasticity

Conditioning can raise resilience because of the brain's neuroplasticity. Neuroplasticity is "the lifelong capacity of the brain to create new neurons (brain cells) and connections among neurons (neural pathways and circuits)" (p. 13). According to Rossouw (2020), brain-derived neurotrophic factor (BDNF) is a protein that helps support learning and adaptability by affecting four types of neuroplasticity:

1. Neurogenesis – The creation of new neurons in the hippocampus improves short-term memory formation.
2. Dendritogenesis – Neurons generate new dendrites, which are arms with synapses extending from the neuron, allowing new neural connections to form.
3. Synaptogenesis – Gene transcription results in new synapses being expressed, providing more sites to connect with other neurons.
4. Synaptic strengthening – The actual strength of synaptic connections change, allowing stronger connection between neurons, leading to long-term learning and adaptation. (para. 6)

All of these forms of neuroplasticity are directly affected by the levels of BDNF in the brain. When in abundance, BDNF speeds up neuroplasticity and improves learning and adaptability. When the hormone cortisol increases in the brain due to stress or trauma, BDNF is diluted, slowing down neuroplasticity and restricting learning and adaptability (Roussow, 2020).

Resilience is therefore empowered with more BDNF. Specific lifestyle factors can contribute directly to raising BDNF levels. These include exercise, quality sleep, healthy nutrition, and engaging versus stressful environments (Roussow, 2020). According to Dym Bartlett and Steber (2019):

> The context in which children live, learn, and grow shapes both their immediate and long-term well-being. Accordingly, children who experience trauma are more likely to exhibit resilience when their environments are responsive to their specific needs. Families, schools, community-based programs and services, and the individuals caring for children can increase the chances of resilience following childhood trauma when they become aware of the impact of childhood trauma, provide a sense of safety and predictability, protect children from further adversity, and offer pathways for their recovery. In other words, children benefit when these entities provide them with trauma-informed care.
>
> (para. 20)

The Case for Trauma-Responsive Discipline

Trauma-responsive discipline is trauma-informed care (TIC). Whereas exclusionary discipline is punitive based and can be stress producing, trauma-responsive discipline builds resilience through secure attachment, conditioning, and neuroplasticity. Interventions that promote prosocial behavior have been proven to have a positive effect on student discipline and achievement.

For example, Durlak et al. (2011) conducted a meta-analysis of 213 social-emotional learning (SEL) programs reaching more than 270,000 children, K-12. Compared with controls who did not receive SEL, student participants demonstrated significant gains in SEL skills, attitudes, and behavior and scored an average of 11% better on standardized measures of achievement. In Chapter 6 (**R**espond), we recommend SEL and other trauma-responsive practices that improve behavior, regulate emotion, and raise resilience. These include multi-tiered systems of supports (MTSS), positive behavioral intervention supports (PBIS), restorative practices (RP), restorative justice (RJ), restorative in-school suspension, de-escalation training, cultural competence training, and mindfulness. We also discuss the critical need for engaging instruction, routines and procedures, family and community engagement, and therapeutic support to be part of a holistic view of discipline throughout a school or school division.

To truly meet the needs of all students, trauma-responsive discipline must be a comprehensive effort that involves school administrators, general education teachers, special education teachers, instructional assistants, school social workers, school psychologists, cafeteria workers, office staff, bus drivers, volunteers, families, "and anyone else who comes in contact with children" (Dym Bartlett & Steber, 2019, para. 21). All educators need to shift their personal narrative when working with challenging students from "What is wrong with you?" to "What happened to you?" (Franck & Chapman, 2018; Sporleder & Forbes, 2016).

Most importantly, trauma-responsive discipline must actively involve students themselves to develop trusting relationships with adults and classmates, learn and use coping skills, and acquire a sense of empathy for others. Ginsburg and Jablow (2020) argue that all students can and must learn to take responsibility for their own actions versus seeing themselves as victims. Resilient children "can be decision-makers and problem-solvers who control outcomes" (p. 315). With adult guidance, reasonable boundaries, evidence-based practices, and love, trauma-responsive discipline can empower all children to empower themselves.

References

Andersen, S. (2016). Commentary on the special issue on the adolescent brain: Adolescence, trajectories, and the importance of prevention. *Neuroscience and Biobehavioral Reviews, 70*, 329–333. doi: 10.1016/j.neubiorev.2016.07.012.

Bartlett, J. D., Smith, S., & Bringewatt, E. (2017). *Helping young children who have experienced trauma: Policies and strategies for early care and education.* Bethesda, MD: Child Trends. Retrieved March 19, 2019 from https://www.chi ldtrends.org/wp-content/uploads/2017/04/2017-19ECETrauma.pdf.

Bath, K., Manzano-Nieves, G., & Goodwill, H. (2016). Hormones and behavior: Early life stress accelerates behavioral and neural maturation of the hippocampus in male mice. *Hormones and Behavior, 82*, 64–71. doi: 10.1016/j.yhbeh.2016.04.010.

Bergland, C. (2013, January). Cortisol: Why the "stress hormone" is public enemy no. 1. *Psychology Today.* Retrieved from https://www.psychologytod ay.com/us/blog/the-athletes-way/201301/cortisol-why-the-stress-hormone -is- public-enemy-no-1.

Bolton, J., Molet, J., Regev, L., Chen, Y., Rismanchi, N., Haddad, E., … Baram, T. (2017). Anhedonia following early-life adversity involves aberrant interaction of reward and anxiety circuits and is reversed by partial silencing of amygdala corticotropin-releasing hormone gene. *Society of Biological Psychiatry, 83*, 137–147. doi: 10.1016/j.biopsych.2017.08.023.

Briere, J. N., & Elliott, D. M. (1994). Immediate and long-term impacts of child sexual abuse. *Future of Children, (4)*2, 54–69. http://www.jstor.org/stable /1602523.

Brown, N., Brown, S., Briggs, R., German, M., Belamarich, P., & Oyeku, S. (2016). Associations between adverse childhood experiences and ADHD diagnosis and severity. *Academic Pediatrics, 17*(4), 349–355. doi: 10.1016/j.acap.2016.12.009.

Burns, S., Szyszkowicz, J., Luheshi, G., & Lutz, P. (2018). Plasticity of the epigenome during early-life stress. *Seminars in Cell & Developmental Biology, 77*, 115–132. doi: 10.1016/j.semcdb.2017.09.033.

Cook, A, Sinazzola, J, Ford, J, Lanktree, C., Blaustein, M., Cloitre, M., … van der Kolk, B. (2005, May). Complex trauma in children and adolescents. *Psychiatric Annals, 35*(5), 390–398.

Durlak, J. A., Weissberg, R. P., Dymnicki, A. B., Taylor, R. D., & Schellinger, K. B. (2011). The impact of enhancing students' social and emotional learning: A meta-analysis of school-based universal interventions. *Child Development, 82*(1), 405–432. doi: 10.1111/j.1467-8624.2010.01564.x.

Dym Bartlett, J., & Steber, K. (2019). *How to implement trauma-informed care to build resilience to childhood trauma.* Bethesda, MD: ChildTrends. Retrieved from https://www.childtrends.org/publications/how-to-implement-trauma-infor med-care-to-build-resilience-to-childhood-trauma.

Fareri, D., & Tottenham, N. (2016). Effects of early life stress on amygdala and striatal development. *Developmental Cognitive Neuroscience, 19*, 233–247.

Felitti, V., Anda, R., Nordenberg, D., Williamson, D., Spitz, A., Edwards, V., … Marks, J. (1998). Relationship to childhood abuse and household dysfunction to many of the leading causes of death in adults: The adverse childhood experiences (ACE) study. *American Journal of Preventive Medicine, 14* (4), 245–258. doi: 10.1016/S0749-3797(98)00017-8.

Franck, L. K., & Chapman, M. (2018). *Trauma and resilience basics.* Presentation sponsored by the Trauma Informed Community Network, Richmond, VA.

Ginsburg, K. (2018). The 7C's: The essential building blocks of resilience. *Fostering Resilience.* Retrieved from http://www.fosteringresilience.com/7cs/php.

Ginsburg, K., & Jablow, M. (2020). *Building resilience in children and teens: Giving kids roots and wings,* 4th ed. Itasca, IL: American Academy of Pediatrics.

Graham, L. (2013). *Bouncing back: Rewiring your brain for maximum resilience and well-being.* Novato, CA: New World Library.

Greeson, J. K. P., Briggs, E. C., Kisiel, C. L., Layne, C. M., Ake III, G. S., Ko, S. J... Fairbank, J. A. (2011). Complex trauma and mental health in children and adolescents placed in foster care: Findings from the National Child Traumatic Stress Network. *Child Welfare, 90*(6), 91–108.

Heim, C., & Binder, E. (2012). Current research trends in early life stress and depression: Review of human studies on sensitive periods, gene-environment interactions, and epigenetics. *Experimental Neurology, 233.* 102–111. doi: 10.1016/j.espneurol.2011.10.032.

Krugers, H., Arp, J., Xiong, H., Kanatsou, S., Lesuis, S., Korosi, A., ... Lucassen, P. (2017). Early life adversity: Lasting consequences for emotional learning. *Neurobiology of Stress, 6,* 14–21. doi: 10.1016/j.ynstr.2016.11.005.

Luthar, S. S., Cicchetti, D., & Becker, B. (2000). The construct of resilience: A critical evaluation and guidelines for future work. *Child Development, 71*(3), 543–562.

Lutz, P., & Turecki, G. (2014). DNA methylation and childhood maltreatment: From animal models to human studies. *Neuroscience, 264,* 142–156. doi: 10.1016/j.neuroscience.2013.07.069.

McClelland, S., Korosi, A., Cope, J., Ivy, A., & Baram, T. (2011). Emerging roles of epigenetic mechanisms in the enduring effects of early-life stress and experience on learning and memory. *Neurobiology of Learning and Memory, 96*(1), 79–88. doi: 10.1016/j.nlm.2011.02.008.

National Scientific Council on the Developing Child. (2014). *Excessive stress disrupts the architecture of the developing Brain.* Working paper no. 3. Updated edition. Retrieved March 19, 2019 from http://www.developingchild.harvard.edu.

Rossouw, J. (2020). Neuroplasticity – Why you should care about your BDNF. Retrieved from https://home.hellodriven.com/neuroplasticity-bdnf-resilience.html.

Seghete, K., DePrince, A., & Banich, M. (2018). Preliminary evidence: Association between initial age of exposure to childhood abuse and cognitive control. *International Society for Traumatic Stress Studies, 3,* 437-447. doi: 10.1002/jts.22290.

Sporleder, J., & Forbes, H. T. (2016). *The trauma-informed school: A step-by-step implementation guide for administrators and school personnel.* Boulder, CO: Beyond Consequences Institute, LLC.

Stevens, J. (2012). Aces too high news. ACEs Connection Network. Retrieved from http://acesttohigh.com/about/.

Teicher, M., Samson, J., Anderson, C., & Ohashi, K. (2016). The effects of childhood maltreatment on brain structure, function and connectivity. *Nature Reviews. Neuroscience, 17*, 652–666. doi: 10.1038/nrn.2016.111.

Woolard, A. (2017). Suspended progress 2017: An update on the state of exclusionary discipline in Virginia's public schools (Research Reports October 2017). Retrieved from https://www.justice4all.org/wp-content/uploads/2016/04/Suspended-Progress-2017.pdf.

World Health Organization. (2020). Violence against children. Retrieved from https ://www.who.int/news-room/fact-sheets/detail/violence-against-children#:~:text =Globally%2C%20it%20is%20estimated%20that,the%20past%20year%20(1).

Zannas, A., & West, A. (2014). Epigenetics and the regulation of stress vulnerability and resilience. *Neuroscience, 264*, 157–170. doi: 10.1016/j. neuroscience.2013.12.003.

3   Setting the Stage for Reform

Given what we know about the ineffectiveness of exclusionary discipline, the impact of trauma on children, and the importance of building resilience, we advocate for teaching students to learn from their mistakes. With support structures in place and faculty/staff in schools who are trained in trauma-responsive practices, students can be taught prosocial and developmentally appropriate behaviors that empower them with resilience and responsibility.

Although not all behavior problems are rooted in trauma, and it is often difficult to determine the etiology of student behaviors, all behavior communicates need (Wood, 2018). School discipline reform, therefore, must be viewed through a holistic lens. Trauma-responsive alternatives to exclusionary discipline provide such a lens. They focus on the whole child. They promote *inclusionary* versus exclusionary discipline within a context and continuum of equity that is currently missing in many public schools. Equity is empowerment, which we believe is the ultimate goal of student discipline.

Equity is Empowerment

To solve the inequities of economic marginalization in schools, Gorski (2018) advocates for a structural versus individualistic approach called *equity literacy*. Equity literacy is "the knowledge and skills educators need to become a threat to the existence of bias and inequity in our spheres of influence" (Gorski, 2018, p. 17). Equity literacy involves more than building student resilience to the effects of economic marginalization, but also cultivating teacher understanding and *"will"* to systematically eliminate economic marginalization itself (p. 17). Gorski (2018) rejects the notion that educators should bolster student "grit" to lift themselves out of poverty; instead, educators should bolster their own grit to provide students "with the access and opportunities afforded their wealthier peers" that build resilience (p. 62). Whereas grit is self-generating from a deficit, resilience is community empowering from an injustice.

Equity literacy underlies how we guide school leaders in the main office and classroom toward embracing trauma-responsive practices that prioritize proactive versus punitive discipline and maximize educational opportunity for *all* students. Our structural approach serves these purposes by integrating three research-based frameworks: John Kotter's Eight-Step Change Model (Kotter, 2012), The Missouri Model: A Developmental Framework for Trauma-Informed Approaches (Missouri Department of Mental Health and Partners, 2014), and the Substance Abuse and Mental Health Services Administration (SAMHSA) Four **R**s (SAMHSA, 2014).

John Kotter's Eight-Step Change Model

Leading schools through a paradigm shift from exclusive to inclusive discipline is a significant undertaking for educational leaders. While there are many research-based models of change theory, we have selected John Kotter's Eight-Step Change Model (Kotter, 2012). Leading change involves vision, planning, intentionality, emotion, resistance, momentum, and time. Kotter's Eight-Step Change Model provides intentional steps to help lead and manage change.

1. **CREATE A SENSE OF URGENCY**. Help others see the need for change through a bold, aspirational opportunity statement that communicates the importance of acting immediately.
2. **BUILD A GUIDING COALITION**. A volunteer army needs a coalition of effective people—born of its own ranks—to guide it, coordinate it, and communicate its activities.
3. **FORM A STRATEGIC VISION**. Clarify how the future will be different from the past and how you can make that future a reality.
4. **COMMUNICATE THE VISION**. Large-scale change can only occur when massive numbers of people understand and rally around a common vision.
5. **EMPOWER OTHERS TO ACT**. Removing barriers such as inefficient processes and hierarchies provides the freedom necessary to work across silos and generate real impact.
6. **GENERATE SHORT-TERM WINS**. Wins are the molecules of results. They must be recognized, collected, and communicated—early and often—to track progress and energize volunteers to persist.
7. **SUSTAIN MOMENTUM**. Press harder after the first successes. Your increasing credibility can improve systems, structures, and policies. Be relentless with initiating change after change until the vision is a reality.
8. **ESTABLISH SYSTEMS AND SUPPORT**. Articulate the connections between the new behaviors and organizational success, making

sure they continue until they become strong enough to replace old habits (Kotter, 2012; Kotter International, 2019).

The Missouri Model: A Developmental Framework for Trauma-Informed Approaches

According to The Missouri Model: A Developmental Framework for Trauma-Informed Approaches, a "trauma-informed approach" is an ongoing organizational change process that takes place through stages along a continuum of implementation (Missouri Department of Mental Health and Partners, 2014).

1. **Trauma-aware** organizations have become aware of how prevalent trauma is and have begun to consider that it might impact their students and staff.
2. **Trauma-sensitive** organizations have begun to explore the principles of trauma-informed care (safety, choice, collaboration, trustworthiness, and empowerment) and work daily to build consensus around the principles, consider implications of adopting principles within the organization, and prepare for the change.
3. **Trauma-responsive** organizations have begun to change their organizational culture to highlight the role of trauma. At all levels of the organization, staff begin re-thinking the routines and infrastructure of the organization.
4. **Trauma-informed** organizations have made trauma-responsive practices the organizational norm. The trauma model has become so accepted and thoroughly embedded that it no longer depends on a few leaders. The organization works with other partners to strengthen collaboration around being trauma-informed (Missouri Department of Mental Health and Partners, 2014, pp. 2–7). Trauma-informed organizations are also those that are staffed with mental health experts (National Child Traumatic Stress Network, Schools Committee, 2017).

Substance Abuse and Mental Health Services Administration (SAMHSA)'s Four Rs

In 2001, Congress created the National Child Traumatic Stress Network (NCTSN) to improve support for children and families impacted by traumatic events (National Child Traumatic Stress Network, Schools Committee, 2017). The NCTSN is administered by the Substance Abuse and Mental Health Services Administration (SAMHSA) and the UCLA-Duke University National Center for Child Traumatic Stress (National

Child Traumatic Stress Network, Schools Committee, 2017). The NCTSN (2017) highlights SAMSHA's Four **R**s of supporting individuals impacted by trauma, which we have aligned below with the Missouri Model and John Kotter's Eight-Steps of Change.

1. **Realize** the impact of trauma. Become trauma-aware by creating a sense of urgency and building a guiding coalition.
2. **Recognize** signs and symptoms of trauma. Become trauma-sensitive by forming and communicating a strategic vision.
3. **Respond** by integrating knowledge about trauma throughout the system. Become trauma-responsive by empowering others to act and generating short term wins.
4. **Resist** re-traumatization by systematizing trauma-informed policies, procedures, and practices. Become trauma-informed by sustaining momentum and establishing systems and supports (National Child Traumatic Stress Network, Schools Committee, 2017, p. 4).

We have used the Four **R**s to organize our research, interview discussions, and professional development suggestions to provide a logical sequence of reforming school discipline practices. Figure 3.1 illustrates our integrated *Discipline Reform Model.*

Figure 3.1 Discipline Reform Model (Kotter, 2012; Missouri Department of Mental Health and Partners, 2014; Substance Abuse and Mental Health Services Administration, 2014)

A Call to Action and Coordination of Efforts

To reform student discipline, school leaders must **R**ealize, **R**ecognize, **R**espond to, and **R**esist the harms of punitive routines, racial bias, poverty, and ACEs. As school leaders ourselves, we understand that the amount of work involved is too daunting to go it alone. Reform is both an action and an objective. It is a movement, a cause, a collective battle of change agents against the status quo toward a common goal. Reform must take place both inside and *outside* the school building among all who understand the negative impacts of exclusionary discipline on children. To date, many superintendents, principals, teachers, staff, and families lack a practical understanding of what childhood trauma is and how to respond to it. Leading a fundamental change in disciplinary practice and protocols for *all* children requires knowledge and a coherent vision that establishes structures to differentiate discipline based on a continuum of needs. Our *Discipline Reform Model* guides this leadership process.

Reform is a collective and ongoing effort, so our *Discipline Reform Model* can also be seen as a continuous cycle of leadership (see Figure 3.2). The more we **R**ealize, **R**ecognize, **R**espond to, and **R**esist the inequities of school discipline, the greater the sense of urgency to implement additional solutions.

- What more can we do in our schools?
- Who else is being marginalized?
- How can we even the playing field for every student in US public schools?

Ultimately, we believe trauma-responsive teachers are the key to reform. According to Barber and Mourshed (2017), "the quality of an education system cannot exceed the quality of its teachers" (p. 16). School divisions must be charged with assessing and addressing the needs of both students and teachers to appropriately solve a complex problem. Success in this regard starts with a deeper understanding of the "why" of student behaviors and the professional development of "how" to address them appropriately. In developing trauma-responsive approaches to student discipline, dedicated teachers must be heard, respected, and compensated for making a world of difference in the lives of children and their families. They also must be provided with models of support and leadership.

We interviewed a variety of practitioners and consultants who have implemented trauma-responsive practices, reduced exclusionary discipline, increased instructional time, improved attendance, and extended family and community engagement. Although our interviewees did not use our *Discipline Reform Model* themselves, we have organized their efforts

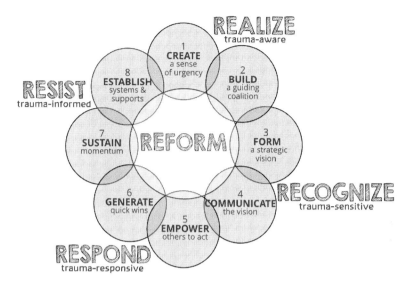

Figure 3.2 Discipline Reform Model in circles (Kotter, 2012; Missouri Department of Mental Health and Partners, 2014; Substance Abuse and Mental Health Services Administration, 2014)

accordingly to provide a more systematic approach for other school leaders to navigate themselves.

Stephanie Poe, one of our authors and the principal of Hopewell High School, Hopewell City Public Schools, is currently implementing our *Discipline Reform Model* with great success!

> My dream is for Hopewell High School to be a place where teachers and students want to be. I dream of a school where the parents are engaged and feel welcome. I am concerned about our student attendance and believe the only way to encourage students to come to school is through relationships. I believe reform towards becoming trauma-responsive will help the faculty and staff build the relationships needed to improve attendance. I worry about the trauma our students experience on a daily basis. It is my hope that establishing a trauma-responsive high school will help move the community towards becoming trauma-responsive. My biggest hope is we will help students build resilience, which will help heal harm that has been experienced in our community.

Ram Bhagat, manager for school culture and climate strategy, Richmond Public Schools, similarly expressed a community need for "equitable and just learning environments for all students." He sees this need for reform as a national crisis.

> Our challenge as a country, if we critically analyze all of our data, reveals we have a national crisis in terms of how we are still dealing with disparities. So many studies illuminate the disparities. When we look at it superficially, it is an indicator of business as usual. We must [instead] address root causes of conflict and how to repair the harm.

Bhagat believes Virginians are "still responding to Massive Resistance (to integrated schools) because we still have intensely racially and financially segregated schools." He expressed concern about the effect of our current system of accountability measures of schools through testing results.

> Our current punitive approach of the accountability movement is where we have kids coming from [racially and financially segregated schools] and we want them to perform on the same level as students who have [multiple] advantages. If they don't, the state is not going to come in with resources to build up, but the state comes in with a gavel to say, "You can't do this, you can't do that, you must do this." It makes it harder to change, and to deal with the effects of those conditions.

Bhagat explained that restorative justice is one way in which Richmond Public Schools can "break down the current mindset." He emphasized first and foremost, "We are a community." Bhagat's hope is for "*Massive Resilience* calling all to action." He wants to restore harm by "building a movement of mindfulness based restorative practices." He shared his desire for Central Virginia schools to work together to become a "lighthouse" to other communities. "We have to make changes in education as a whole if we want to make things happen."

Allison Sampson-Jackson, CEO, Integration Solutions, Inc., is making connections with transformational leaders across the state of Virginia in her role as an educational consultant. For trauma-responsive practices to become a priority for every school, she believes the accountability system needs reform. Currently, accountability measures include standardized test scores and graduation rates. Sampson-Jackson has been exploring ways to measure the effectiveness of trauma-responsive practices such as social-emotional learning curricula. She wants to provide hard data to show legislators how these programs work and to lobby for state funding of SEL supports.

John Richardson-Lauve, director of mental health, Childsavers, also identified standardized testing as a barrier to successful implementation of trauma-responsive practices. He mentioned the need for funding and support of measurable trauma-responsive supports. "Anything that is not on a budget line item is not very important. So we have to make sure there is accountability and then resources." Richardson-Lauve sees the need for reform of teacher and administrator licensure requirements to include information about ACEs and the impact trauma can have on behavior, learning, and mental wellness. However, Richardson-Lauve believes trauma-awareness is growing nationally.

> The ideal is to get to the point where we don't need a trauma-informed initiative or resiliency-based initiative. It's just something that we acknowledge and talk about as something that exists within every IEP meeting, within every behavioral support meeting, within every staff meeting. If we acknowledge it and honor it, we will work to mitigate trauma and build resilience.

Lauren Watts, school counselor, Chesterfield County Public Schools, wants teaching programs to include more instruction and course work in the area of tiered supports and interventions with an emphasis on supporting students impacted by trauma. She also advocates for more counselors in schools.

Connie Honsinger, behavioral intervention specialist, Chesterfield County Public Schools, also believes well-trained teachers, when combined with clearly defined trauma-responsive expectations and procedures, are the key to implementing this much-needed culture shift in our schools. Demonstrating this commitment, she recently published a manuscript in the *Teacher Educators' Journal* titled, "Preparing Trauma-Sensitive Teachers: Strategies for Teacher Educators."

Melissa McGinn, community programs coordinator and coordinator of the Greater Richmond Trauma Informed Community Network (GR-TICN), Stop Child Abuse Now (GR-SCAN), emphasized that the most important part of the process is the community collaboration. A backbone organization is necessary for sustainability, but community collaboration and collective voice is most vital to immediate and long-term success. These networks break down silos and have the ability to coordinate efforts of different systems working together on a shared vision of building a more resilient community.

Denise Powers, lead teacher, Circle Preschool, GR-SCAN, emphasized that a paradigm shift needs to occur in how we look at student discipline overall. Educators "should not look for what is wrong with the student or why the student is choosing to behave this way." Instead, educators should consider "what has happened" and how we can help. Powers noted the local GR-TICN, through GR-SCAN, has been able to pass legislation that requires educators to identify and report child abuse. She and her GR-SCAN colleagues are working to effect policy changes to require pre-service training in trauma-responsiveness. She believes the biggest need for reform is to have more public early childhood programs with integrated therapeutic support.

> If students are not socially or emotionally regulated, which are the impacts of trauma, then we need to provide spaces and time [to teach students to self-regulate]. Students who attend Circle Preschool have not been successful in other preschool or childcare programs because of their behaviors related to trauma. What does it do to a child when they have been kicked out and they say, "I got kicked out, I cannot go [to preschool or childcare] anymore." The message students get at ages three, four, or five is that they have already failed at school.

The eventuality of many more students experiencing a sense of failure in elementary, middle, and high school reinforces the critical importance of providing mental health support in schools, PreK through 12. Powers believes we need to stop blaming students, families, or teachers. "Solving the problem through reform needs to be a community effort." Her wisdom speaks to the politics of reform.

The Politics of Reform

We believe reform must extend far beyond the classroom. Local and state leaders need to prioritize and fund mental health supports and staffing in schools and communities. While many new state laws mandate that school divisions significantly limit exclusionary discipline by eliminating zero-tolerance policies, most do not yet fund the necessary resources to implement alternatives (Gilbreath, 2018; Woolard, 2017). Neither do they provide the professional development necessary to guide restorative discipline of students whose behavior may result from childhood trauma.

In Virginia, laws limiting out-of-school suspension (OSS) have popular support. In 2017, the Virginia General Assembly passed, and Governor Terry McAuliffe signed into law SB829/HB1924, "bills that directed the Virginia Board of Education to establish guidelines for alternatives to suspension and expulsion for consideration by local school boards" (Woolard, 2017, p. 10). In 2018, The Virginia Legislature wrote and Governor Ralph Northam signed two additional school suspension bills. Upon signing these bills, Governor Northam declared, "There is power in every child. We want to keep our children in school" (Mattingly, 2018, para. 9).

Limiting suspensions legislatively in Virginia and elsewhere is a politically expedient means to mandate alternatives to out-of-school exclusionary discipline. Providing school divisions and individual schools with the knowledge and resources to systematically meet these mandates is another matter. By 2017, 27 states had preceded Virginia in passing laws to significantly reduce suspensions and expulsions, while more than 50 large city school districts had reformed their discipline policies to mandate alternatives to exclusionary discipline (Kamenetz, 2017). Like suspensions, these mandates have in some cases proven to be more punitive than productive; they articulate the need for change but do not adequately provide the skills or resources to employ it. Consequently, schools are left with only mandates to develop alternatives to exclusionary discipline or risk non-accreditation. Examples from other states show that when schools are ill-equipped to develop these alternatives, teachers may find themselves in chaotic classrooms.

St. Paul Public Schools

In 2013, St. Paul (Minnesota) Public Schools reduced suspension rates 30% by removing *continual willful disobedience*, deemed too subjective a conduct code, from the district's list of violations for which students can be suspended, and by making bonus pay available to principals who lowered suspension numbers (Lonetree, 2013). In some St. Paul schools, the policy effectively "changed the conversation" about school discipline to "focus on what causes a student to misbehave, and to finding ways to resolve it" (Lonetree, 2017, para. 12). In others, the policy made both teachers and students feel unsafe. "Students have now caught on that suspensions are rare even for serious offenses," said one fifth-grade teacher. Another teacher echoed this concern. "We can't teach kids that are sent out of the room or suspended, so that's the last thing we want. But we also can't teach in a chaotic learning environment" (Lonetree, 2017, para. 7).

Highline Public Schools

Between 2013 and 2016, Highline Public Schools, a racially diverse district south of Seattle, Washington, dramatically reduced suspensions and expulsions by over 74%. Highline Public Schools achieved a 16.5% overall rise in graduation rates over the same period, with 25% more Hispanic students and 22% more Black students graduating on time (D'Orio, 2018). The district provided many high school teachers with coaching in restorative practices, all school staff received at least three hours of training in working with students who had experienced trauma, and all elementary and middle schools were using a Yale University researched program (RULER) to teach social and emotional learning to all of their students.

Yet even with considerable district-wide support in place, reducing out-of-school suspensions (OSSs) by 74% did not necessarily translate to reducing the accompanying misconduct. The number of in-school suspensions (ISSs) rose by over 65% during this same period. One teacher said students became more disrespectful after the threat of OSS had diminished. "Kids will cuss you out, there's stealing and disobedience" (D'Orio, 2018, para. 20). Another teacher noted that one of her students was suspended in-school for three days after throwing a chair across the room, an offense that previously warranted OSS. "The line keeps moving," she complained of the chaos in her classroom (D'Orio, 2018, para. 21). She was not alone in her discontent; 12.7% of the district's roughly 1,400 teachers left the district in 2015 and 2016, an attrition rate that exceeded the national average of 8%, and Highline's rate of 9.6% from 2012–2013 to 2014–2015 (D'Orio, 2018). Squeezed between supporting their teachers and answering to central office, several Highline principals were also accused of lowering their OSS data by simply sending students home without formally logging in these suspensions (D'Orio, 2018).

New York City Public Schools

From 2011 to 2016, New York City Public Schools reduced OSSs by 46% (Zimmerman, 2016). The city attributed the decline to a variety of factors, including a revision of the code of conduct to severely limit suspendable offenses, increased training in restorative justice practices and conflict resolution, and hiring additional counselors and mental health consultants (Zimmerman, 2016). Despite the city's touted success in this regard, union officials complained that de-escalation training for teachers was insufficient and classrooms had become chaotic. United Federation of Teachers (UFT) President Michael Mulgrew stated, "Teachers at a few schools say their principals won't give suspensions even when warranted, inviting some students to act out and threatening their peers' learning and even safety" (Wall, 2016, para. 10). In a letter to New York City Public Schools' Chancellor Carmen Farina, Mulgrew wrote:

> The "Zero-Tolerance" policies of the previous administration clearly backfired—they never led to a nurturing school culture or even-handled discipline. At the same time, we do not believe a 180-degree pivot banning suspensions makes sense unless schools have the necessary supports and interventions in place...It is easy to ban suspensions. It is much harder to do the real work so suspensions are no longer necessary.
>
> (United Federation of Teachers, 2016, para. 3–4)

More Than Legislative Mandates

These districts are just three school divisions who are making significant ongoing progress with discipline reform. However, their early experiences demonstrate how the problem of exclusionary discipline requires more than legislative mandates. A top-down approach to disciplinary reform overlooks and underestimates what needs to take place in individual schools and school divisions to become restorative versus reactionary. While mandates alone may lower suspension rates, they raise anxiety about safety and security among students, parents, teachers, and principals. In-school suspensions, like OSSs, may also exacerbate the behaviors they intend to correct if students perceive them as wholly punitive, not punitive at all, or unresponsive to the underlying causes of their behavior. And if teachers perceive their classrooms as chaotic, they may abandon the profession. High expectations and accountability should not be removed from trauma-responsive discipline. They must be directly taught. Instruction in trauma-responsive discipline practice requires funding for ongoing professional development, smaller class sizes, multi-tiered interventions by trained staff, and time to teach research-based social and emotional learning (SEL) curricula.

To effectively address the problem of exclusionary discipline, lawmakers must legislate solutions that support students and teachers alike. Legal Aid Justice Center provides several primary recommendations that are student-centered, school-based, and school-supportive.

- Enact legislation that limits the use and duration of suspension and expulsion.
- Require the continued provision of free, high-quality education for all students removed or reassigned from public K-12 classrooms or schools for disciplinary reasons.
- Collect and report data, disaggregated by race, sex, grade, and disability, on alternative education programs provided by local school divisions to students subjected to disciplinary measures like suspension and reassignment.
- Develop and implement a comprehensive plan to address and eliminate race and disability disparities.
- Lift constraints on school support staff positions, most especially school counselors, social workers, psychologists, and nurses.
- Direct adequate resources into proven alternatives to suspension and expulsion, like restorative practices, multi-tiered systems of supports, and SEL programs.
- Local school divisions, community partners, parents, and students should engage with one another in designing codes of conduct to

reframe school discipline in ways that focus on strengthening students and schools, rather than defaulting to punishment and isolation. (Woolard, 2018, pp. 11–14)

Facilitating a systemic shift in mindset from punitive to trauma-responsive discipline practices must also include **R**ealizing, **R**ecognizing, and **R**esponding to trauma, and **R**esisting retraumatization. Currently, the majority of schools do not have designated mental health professionals to provide trauma-informed supports. While school psychologists, social workers, and other mental health providers may be integrated into supports for students, full-time positions are rarely funded at the individual school level (Cole et al., 2009; Wolpow, Johnson, Hertel, & Kincaid, 2009). To help schools be more trauma-responsive, state governments should reduce the ratio of trauma-informed counselors to students and teachers as recommended by the American School Counselor Association (ASCA). Over a 10-year period (2004–2014), the national ratio of school counselors to students was 482:1; ASCA recommends a 250:1 student-to-counselor ratio and cites only three states (New Hampshire, Vermont, and Wyoming) that maintained a ratio lower than 250:1 (National Association for College Admission Counseling (NACAC) and the ASCA, 2016, para. 4).

Additionally, practical recommendations should accompany policy recommendations. Faced with mandates to provide alternatives to exclusionary discipline, principals need professional guidance to identify and implement successful discipline alternatives for students. Principals require networking and models of how to lead a structured paradigm shift from punitive to positive discipline in their schools. Principals also must have equitable access in all corners of their states to trauma-informed resources for their students, teachers, and staff.

Our book offers many answers and additional questions to ask. So let's get started with **R**ealizing the mission ahead.

References

Barber, M., & Mourshed, M. (2017). How the world's best performing school systems come out top. (Research Report, September 2, 2017). Retrieved from https://www.mckinsey.com/industries/social-sector/our-insights/how-the-worlds-best-performing-school-systems-come-out-on-top.

Cole, S. F., O'Brien, J. G., Gadd, M. G., Ristuccia, J., Wallace, D. L., & Gregory, M. (2009). *Helping traumatized children learn: Supportive school environments for children traumatized by family violence.* Boston, MA: Massachusetts Advocates for Children.

D'Orio, W. (2018, January 11). Is school-discipline reform moving too fast? *The Atlantic*. Retrieved from https://www.theatlantic.com/education/archive/2018/01/is-school-discipline-reform-moving-too-fast/550196/.

Gilbreath, A. (2018). 2018 Legislative session: Dismantling the school-to-prison pipeline. *Voices for Virginia's Children*. Retrieved from https://vakids.org/our-news/blog/2018-legislative-session-dismantling-the-school-to-prison-pipeline

Gorski, P. C. (2018). *Reaching and teaching students in poverty: Strategies for erasing the opportunity gap*, 2nd ed. New York: Teachers' College Press.

Kamenetz, A. (2017). School suspensions have plunged: We don't know yet if that's good news. *NPREd*. Retrieved from https://www.npr.org/sections/ed/2017/03/23/521070924/school-suspensions-have-plunged-we-don-t-yet-know-if-that-s-good-news

Kotter, J. P. (2012). *Leading change*. Boston, MA: Harvard Business School Press.

Kotter International. (2019). *Kotter*. Retrieved from https://www.kotterinc.com/8-steps-process-for-leading-change/.

Lonetree, A. (2013, May 23). St. Paul school suspensions drop 30%: Administrators make clear an intent to keep students in the classroom. *Star Tribune*. Retrieved from http://www.startribune.com/st-paul-school-suspensions-drop-30/208760501/.

Mattingly, J. (2018). Northam signs student discipline reform bill as Virginia schools still disproportionately suspend black students. *Richmond Times Dispatch*. Retrieved from https://www.richmond.com/news/virginia/government-politics/general-assembly/northam-signs-student-discipline-reform-bills-as-virginia-schools-still/article_ee156e85-43b8-59ce-be13-e767818e9b91.html

Missouri Department of Mental Health and Partners (2014). *Missouri model: A developmental framework for trauma informed approaches*. Retrieved from https://dmh.mo.gov/trauma/MO%20Model%20Working%20Document%20february%202015. pdf.

National Association for College Admission Counseling and the American School Counselor Association. (2016). State by state student to counselor ratio report: 10-year trends. Retrieved from https://www.schoolcounselor.org/asca/media/asca/Publications/ratioreport.pdf.

National Child Traumatic Stress Network, Schools Committee. (2017). *Creating, supporting, and sustaining trauma-informed schools: A system framework*. Los Angeles, CA: National Center for Child Traumatic Stress.

Substance Abuse and Mental Health Services Administration. (2014). *Guiding principles of trauma-informed care. 22*(2). Retrieved from https://www.samhsa.gov/samhsaNewsLetter/Volume_22_Number_2/trauma_tip/guiding_principles.html.

United Federation of Teachers. (2016). UFT responds to the DOE's ban on suspensions in the early grades. [Press Release]. Retrieved from http://www.uft.org/press-releases/uft-responds-does-ban-suspensions-students-early-grades.

Wall, P. (2016, April 20). As New York City's suspension rate falls, some educators see a parallel dip in discipline. *Chalkbeat*. Retrieved from https://www.chalkbeat.org/posts/ny/2016/04/20/as-new-york-citys-suspension-rate-falls-some-educators-see-a-parallel-dip-in-discipline/.

Wolpow, R., Johnson, M. M., Hertel, R., & Kincaid, S. O. (2009). *The heart of teaching and learning: Compassion, resiliency, and academic success.* Olympia, WA: Washington State Office of Superintendent of Public Instruction Compassionate Schools.

Wood, L. (2018, November). Putting resiliency understanding to work for youth (and you). In S. Dion (Chair), *Strengthening connections: Fostering resiliency and supporting the development of safe and healthy students from kindergarten through college.* Symposium conducted at the meeting of the Virginia Department of Criminal Justice Services, Richmond, VA.

Woolard, A. (2017). Suspended progress 2017: An update on the state of exclusionary discipline in Virginia's public schools (Research Reports October 2017). Retrieved From https://www.justice4all.org/wp-content/uploads/2016/04/Suspended-Progress-2017.pdf.

Woolard, A., Salas, M., & Deane, R. (2018). Suspended progress, 2018: An update on the state of exclusionary discipline and alternative education in Virginia's public schools (Research Reports October 2018). Retrieved from https://www.justice4all.org/wpcontent/uploads/2018/10/FullSuspendedProgress2018.pdf.

Zimmerman, A. (2016, October 31). New York City school suspensions continue to plummet, but stark disparities exist. Chalkbeat. Retrieved from https://www.chalkbeat.org/posts/ny/2016/10/31/new-york-city-school-suspensions-continue-to-plummet-but-stark-disparities-persist/.

Part II
Leading Trauma-Responsive Discipline Reform

4 Realize
Developing a Schoolwide Awareness of Trauma

Realizing trauma means becoming *trauma-aware*. Trauma-aware organizations "have become aware of how prevalent trauma is and have begun to consider that it might impact their [students] and staff" (Missouri Department of Mental Health and Partners, 2014, p. 2). Becoming a trauma-aware school is a transformation that should begin with *creating a sense of urgency* and *building a guiding coalition* (Kotter, 2012).

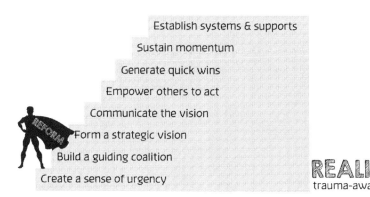

Figure 4.1 Discipline Reform Model: REALIZE (Kotter, 2012; Missouri Department of Mental Health and Partners, 2014; Substance Abuse and Mental Health Services Administration, 2014)

Role of the Principal

While teachers are the most important component in helping students achieve their potential as learners, "teachers attest that the most important person in facilitating [student] achievement…is the principal" (Lumpkin, 2008, p. 24). The role of the principal is vital to the culture of a school and critical to leading trauma-awareness.

Principals create a sense of urgency by sharing information which encourages followers to believe in the need for change. Each of the leaders we interviewed described different reasons and processes for establishing the sense of urgency within their schools or school systems. Common threads included equity concerns, discipline practices which were not changing behavior (particularly zero-tolerance policies), increased student behavioral issues, a desire to improve school culture and climate, and an awareness of the need to teach social-emotional skills to all students.

Principals must build a guiding coalition to "guide, coordinate, and communicate the activities" as a school becomes trauma-aware (Kotter, 2012). The guiding coalition should be members from the school community who are influential and passionate about student discipline reform. The leaders we interviewed suggested members of the guiding coalition should include some or all of the following: the principal, other school administrators, teacher leaders, district-level leaders and specialists, school social workers and psychologists, school counselors, educational consultants, mental health professionals, parents, and students when developmentally appropriate. Guiding coalitions are often called Trauma-Informed Leadership Teams (TILTs) because they have some members who are trauma-informed.

Steps to Becoming Trauma-Aware

First, the guiding coalition should read and discuss the following sections of this book to identify your school's sense of urgency:

- Introduction (**Redefine**): What is your current working definition of student discipline?
- Chapter 1 (**Review**): What problems with exclusionary discipline resonate within your school community?
- Chapter 2 (**Refocus**): How do the lenses of trauma and resilience refocus your approach to student discipline?
- Chapter 3 (**Reform**): How does your school's approach to student discipline need structural Reform?

Second, the guiding coalition should dive into annual school discipline data to uncover objective trends in student behaviors and administrative consequences.

- What disruptive behaviors are most prevalent in your school?
- How many suspensions did you have last year and for which offenses?

- Do you notice any racial or gender disparities?
- Are the same individual students repeatedly being disciplined?
- What other approaches have been tried with these students?

Third, each member of your guiding coalition should take a personal inventory using the survey Realizing Trauma-Awareness (Appendix A). Compare your scores individually and collectively as you discuss the following:

- For what reasons might some of you be more trauma-aware than others?
- What personal experiences have made you trauma-aware?
- Which of these questions challenged you and why?
- How does learning about trauma affect your view of student discipline?

Fourth, the guiding coalition should collectively take the survey on behalf of the staff to estimate the overall level of trauma-awareness within the school or division. The survey can also be given directly to staff. Results will guide your selection of resources to develop trauma-awareness.

Finally, thoroughly explore the professional development resources at the end of this chapter. Depending upon your school needs, you may want to watch and discuss the documentary *Resilience*, or Dr. Nadine Burke Harris's Ted Talk (both are briefly described at the end of this chapter). We highly recommend playing *The Brain Architecture Game* with your staff (also described). Each school is unique, so your school's level of urgency, approach, and time devoted should be individualized. Your group may also want to consult other resources for more information and professional development on implicit bias, microaggressions, and culturally responsive instruction.

As you plan professional development for your staff, you should consider the following:

- Know your faculty, staff, students, and community.
- Plan for ongoing professional development and follow-up (no "one-and-dones").
- Due to the sensitivity of the content, partnering with trauma-informed experts from your school division or community to deliver content is recommended.
- Becoming trauma-aware is a process (a marathon, not a sprint). Be intentional and choose resources that will resonate with your school community.

Realizing the Need for Family and Community Engagement

The guiding coalition should also **R**ealize the need to create a sense of urgency for reformed practices with families. Asking families how they would like to learn about ACEs can inform decisions about how, when, and where to disseminate the information. Some communities have sponsored public viewings of the documentary *Resilience* to begin the conversation. Other schools have presented at monthly Parent Teacher Associations to disseminate the information. It is important that teachers and administrators talk openly with parents and guardians about individual discipline concerns and trends in your school both privately and publicly.

- How can you partner together to address antisocial student behaviors through means other than exclusionary discipline?
- How can you communicate a **R**ealization that behavior communicates need (e.g., attention seeking, misunderstanding, frustration, anxiety, chronic stress, etc.)?
- How can you empower parents to help turn negative attention-seeking student behavior to positive attention-seeking student behavior?

In some cases, school leaders need to think strategically about who is the right person from the community to deliver sensitive information about ACEs. Schools need to find ways to deliver the information to avoid portraying school personnel as the experts and families are passive recipients, or that experts are there judging them.

Schools also need to **R**ealize that the definition of family is no longer the traditional two parent home. Deliberately shifting language from parent involvement to *family engagement* implies all families are welcome partners to improve student outcomes. A critical thing to **R**ealize about family engagement is that the purpose is *not* to get parents to value their child's education more. According to Gorski (2018), dozens of studies have shown since the 1970s families experiencing poverty share the same attitudes about the value of education as wealthier families. The purpose of family engagement is to break down barriers and make resources, programs, and partnership more accessible to families (Gorski, 2018). Some families may not be able to attend school programs during the day, may not have transportation, or may speak a different language than the predominant language in the school. And while families may not have an awareness of trauma, they certainly may have an interest in learning about it as it affects those they love.

Leading Realization

To assist with leading trauma-awareness, we share stories and lessons learned from school leaders and trauma-informed experts who have helped their school communities become trauma-aware. None of the professionals we interviewed began this work with a complete understanding of how to create a trauma-aware school community. Most were learning along the way and shared their efforts towards helping individuals Realize how trauma happens, what the effects of trauma can be, and the relationships between trauma, student behavior, and adult actions. The catalyst for taking action and the path taken to create a trauma-aware school community also varied greatly.

Once the leaders Realized the significance of the impact of trauma in their schools, they began the process of sharing this information with their staff and communities. Through data, experts, committees, teams, community organizations, staffing, and/or professional development, they created a sense of urgency and developed guiding coalitions to lead trauma-awareness. It is our hope that their stories guide and inspire you as school leaders to help all stakeholders within your community to become trauma-aware.

A High School Principal Realizes

Stephanie Poe, a co-author of this book, became principal of Hopewell High School in Hopewell, Virginia, while completing research for her dissertation. She was eager to help her staff Realize the effects of trauma on student learning and behaviors. She first shared information about trauma with the assistant principals, who quickly Realized many of their students were exhibiting behaviors commonly displayed by students affected by trauma. The administrative team began discussing the neuroscience related to chronic stress, and together Realized the urgency to become a trauma-aware school. One assistant principal stated, "It's a brave leap, but much needed."

The administrative team began planning for pre-service professional development. They began the year by watching both *Paper Tigers* and *Resilience*. The documentaries led to discussions comparing Hopewell High school to the school in *Paper Tigers*. They discussed ways in which Jim Sporleder, principal of Lincoln High School in Walla Walla, Washington, was able to change the culture of the school from a punitive to productive environment.

The day after showing the videos, one of the football coaches shared a story with the faculty about applying with a player what he had learned in the training the previous afternoon. The player was clearly exhibiting some of the behaviors portrayed in the video. The coach admitted he would have typically yelled at the player or sent him away from the field, maybe even home for the day. Instead, he decided to respond by talking with the player and giving him a chance to take a break before returning to practice. The coach shared his amazement with how well the player responded and how the coach felt the change made for a better relationship and practice.

An Elementary School Staff Realizes

When *Joshua Cole* was appointed principal of Ecoff Elementary, Chesterfield County Public Schools (CCPS), he maintained a strong focus on academics, particularly state assessments, while adhering to the zero-tolerance discipline practices in place. Cole spent time observing the culture of the school and consulted with a variety of stakeholders, including teachers, parents, community members, and students, while also completing his own research on social-emotional learning (SEL). His research included reading relevant literature such as *Help For Billy* by Heather Forbes and attending conferences focused on SEL. Following his observations and research, Cole Realized the need to develop supports for students impacted by trauma. He concluded, "Students cannot focus on academics and learning if they are not emotionally stable."

Cole used school student data to help faculty and staff gain a sense of urgency to become trauma-aware. Realizing that poverty can be a contributing factor to trauma, Cole shared data on the significant increase in the number of economically disadvantaged children attending Ecoff Elementary. Between 2011 and 2017, the percentage of students receiving a free lunch had increased from 30% to 49%. In 2016, the number of Ecoff students who were suspended had grown to an all-time high of 58 suspensions, a data point Cole considered unacceptable.

Cole consulted CCPS behavioral intervention specialist *Connie Honsinger*, who became a tremendous resource for Ecoff Elementary. She helped the leadership team to Realize that behavior was an expression of need, and that the staff had to become trauma-aware before they could be trauma-responsive.

> [I needed to help create] a mindset shift of viewing behavior from a different lens while considering the impact of trauma on our students. Many students with challenging behaviors have developed these patterns as attempts to cope with often toxic levels of stress. We have to consider how we can meet their needs rather than just focusing on modifying their behavior. In order to provide equitable environments for all students we must consider the impact of trauma.

Honsinger shared her philosophy of "understanding before helping: with leadership, faculty, and staff" at 50 CCPS schools. She showed the *ACEs Primer* video (see PD resources) to introduce faculties to ACEs and the significant impact trauma can have on a student's achievement, social-emotional well-being, and behavior. Honsinger personally *Realized* she captured the attention of her audience by focusing on the neuroscience of the impacts of trauma. After the neuroscience is explained, "faculty and staff have found it nearly impossible to debate or question the importance of supporting students impacted by trauma." Honsinger quoted Dan Siegel, author of the book *Healing Trauma*, "You have to be able to name it to tame it" (2010). Once having "named" trauma, she explained, faculty and staff can shift their focus to actually creating a trauma-responsive environment.

A Preschool Program Realizes

Denise Powers, lead teacher, Circle Preschool (GR-SCAN), believes that trauma-awareness must first begin with the **R**ealization that a zero-tolerance approach is illogical. "Students at public schools come to school with trauma and act out, then they are punished for trauma-related behaviors." Circle Preschool serves students between the ages of three and five. Powers shared, "All of our students have experienced trauma and some of them have IEPs. [None of the students] ha[s] been able to remain in childcare or preschool settings, often because of acting out behaviors. Others have not had the opportunity to have these early educational experiences."

Students in Circle Preschool are identified by family members, the Department of Social Services, Child Protective Services, or other GR-SCAN programs. Powers expressed concern about the difficulty in finding enough qualified trained teachers, which thereby limits the number of students they can serve. This challenge may indicate that few teachers ever receive adequate trauma-awareness training. "It is extremely hard work to help the brain rewire and to see what young children have endured." Powers explained they are very open and honest when hiring and will ask interviewees, "What would it be like if a child spits in your face? What will you do with that strong feeling?" She also explained they spend significant time "training staff to be prepared" to handle their own strong feelings.

Powers is part of a team that utilizes play-based learning and therapy based on the Reggio Emilia Approach, which focuses on critical thinking and collaboration. "Educators develop curricula based on each child's specific interests, emphasizing both the environment in which a child learns, and the social environment created by caregivers, staff, and peers" (GR-SCAN, 2019, para. 9). Powers shared her passion for teaching social-emotional school readiness and for replicating this approach in preschool programs throughout Virginia and elsewhere. "Many children cannot reach their potential because of all the hindrances of trauma and poverty. This is a generational challenge, but no one wants to be stuck in the cycle of abuse."

A Small School Division Realizes

Patrick Farrell, behavior support specialist, Charlottesville City Schools (CCS), described a number of factors as the impetus for CCS's transition to become more trauma-aware. "We were seeing increasingly intense behavior, way too many kids were being put into alternative settings, and generational layers of people having unsatisfactory experiences at school. There isn't an all-consuming trust in the community…some people don't feel that warm and fuzzy." The White nationalist Unite the Right Rally in Charlottesville on August 12, 2017, reinvigorated the division's commitment to re-establishing trust and pride between the community and the division. Farrell explained the division leaders posited, "How can we be a lot more intentional and responsive within CCS, and then how can we rebuild those connections to the community?"

Farrell explained that Title IV grant funds allowed the division to invest in professional development and materials. "They started with division-wide professional development to increase awareness about the potential impact of trauma on students. By exposing all teachers to the science behind ACEs at a county-wide convocation, 'Aha' moments created rippling effects within each building." Farrell called trauma-awareness "the low hanging fruit" and cautioned, "If you have the skillset, but you don't have the mindset, these things are not going to be effective."

We talked with participants from Clark Elementary in CCS to understand what happened after the county-wide professional development. They told us they were motivated to transform classroom practices because of what they had learned and had experienced at Clark Elementary. *Kathryn Grant*, teacher of four-year-olds, **R**ealized, "We had kids who had behaviors that were problematic and intractable," and she told us that the strategies she had used in the past were not working. *Kelly Bullock,* teacher of three-year-olds, **R**ealized, "I think we always kind of knew [about the impact of trauma] but we never really called it trauma till then." *Dana Carrico*, teacher of three-year-olds, **R**ealized, "It gave us a name and that was the beginning for me to look at [student behavior] in a different way."

A Large Suburban School Division Realizes

Upon her appointment in 2014, *Nyah Hamlett*, assistant superintendent for instructional support, Henrico County Public Schools (HCPS), **R**ealized the need to analyze the division's discipline data from a different lens due to disproportionality in exclusionary discipline. She began by looking at district suspension data and found that in 2009–2010, the year with the highest number of suspensions, there were over 10,000 out-of-school suspensions. "This translated to over 70,000 hours of missed instructional time," Hamlett explained, a statistic she used to illustrate the urgency of changing the division's approach to discipline.

"We really started digging deeper," said Hamlett, "and we started looking at the number of suspensions that were given to students for 'D code' violations." Hamlett explained that D code violations, Disrespect, Defiance, and Disruption, were disproportionate among Black students and students with disabilities (SWD) in HCPS. Beyond justifying urgency, data from schools with the most "D Code" violations was used to identify where Hamlett would focus professional development, student supports, and a guiding coalition that included behavioral support specialists.

William Noel, Sr., director of student support and disciplinary review, said "D Codes" are the highest overall conduct code violations countywide. He emphasized the continued urgency for "going deeper to reach the sometimes hard to reach." He believes teachers can better understand students if they are personally aware of implicit bias, poverty, and trauma.

> You want to be culturally proficient. It's that simple. If you know the student's story, you're better equipped to deal with him. If you know your student is from poverty, if you know your student has been abused, or your student has a mental illness, or [his/her] parents are incarcerated, you will treat those students equitably versus equally. I think that is incredibly important if you're going to reach them. It's more important to know who you teach than what you teach.

Having a deep level of student awareness has been a foundational principle as Noel and his team work closely with administrators, teachers, parents, and students.

An Urban School Division Realizes

Ram Bhagat, manager of school culture and climate strategy, Richmond Public Schools (RPS), emphasized how important it is "to understand the principles and philosophies first." "Trauma is universal and there is very little difference between [types of] schools. We have a lot to learn [because] we are all affected by it [and we need to determine] how we can deal with it." Bhagat continued by sharing the concern that school staff members often contribute to the trauma, especially in high poverty schools.

So many of our kids are coming from communities saturated with traumatogenic (trauma causing) factors and the first thing they do [at school] is go through a metal detector. [Why is it] kids at another school, where there is a higher probability of a shooting do not have to go through a metal detector? What we want is a conflict of paradigms. We want students to sit still, listen, sit up straight, be quiet, 'no, you can't get water', etc…yet we want engagement, happiness, listening, obedience.

Bhagat believes the paradigms of educational expectations must change. Bhagat started with "coalition of the willing" leadership teams, which consist of administrative teams at three middle schools. "[The schools] were identified because their principals were passionate about embarking on the mission." The "coalition of the willing" began by participating in after school professional development regarding trauma-informed practices. "The coalition also participated in intensive immersion training (a 14-hour training) on [restorative] circle processes, specifically, community building circles." Later, the coalition participated in "advanced peacemaking circle training" with Kay Pranis, author of *Little Book of Circle Processes* and co-author of *Circle Forward*. Participants were eager to bring what they learned back to their own schools.

Margo Buchanan, resiliency project coordinator, RPS, and trauma-informed child and family therapist, GR-SCAN, explained how she coordinated professional development at eight RPS schools within one high school feeder pattern. With the help of ChildSavers, a licensed mental health provider was staffed to embed professional development at Martin Luther King, Jr. Middle School in 2017, with additional elementary schools to follow. The professional development and clinicians provided to RPS were the result of a collaborative effort as multiple organizations provided funding and support. These included the Children's Memorial Foundation, Impact 100, Bon Secours, and Richmond Public School Foundation. All clinicians received extensive training on trauma-responsive practices, and most have had previous experience working in the school setting. Buchanan said the work of GR-SCAN primarily rests in the **R**ealize phase as it simply takes time to help faculty and staff become aware that many of us have emotional challenges, but "we all respond differently." Responses differ based on "experience, temperament, trust, and relationships."

Buchanan emphasized that the implementation of a Trauma-Informed Leadership Team (TILT) is vital when working toward becoming a trauma-responsive school. Buchanan explained that the purpose of the TILT is to help the entire school transition through the four **R**s. She suggested if school administrators are struggling to find teachers and leaders to serve on the TILT, it may be a sign that the staff is not ready to begin implementation. Instead, school leaders may need to regroup to focus on helping a select number of faculty and staff **R**ealize what trauma is and how it may impact students.

Olivya Wilson, RPS resiliency project parent engagement coordinator, GR-SCAN, works within RPS to provide professional development designed to raise awareness of trauma through a family engagement lens. While helping faculty and staff build authentic relationships, Wilson focuses on "identifying biases that may have developed over the course of time as a teacher at a specific school within a specific community." One of Wilson's tasks is to help faculty **R**ealize biases exist which may shape how they view and interact with students and families.

Wilson challenges faculty to dig deeper when meeting with families to discuss student concerns or observations. She encourages teachers to consider potential traumatic circumstances that may impact the student or family. "Don't just assume a parent who does not attend a conference or participate in a school event does not care." She explained the reason for the lack of family participation may be the result of other circumstances, such as working a second job. Prior to receiving professional development in parent engagement through a trauma-aware lens, teachers are often unaware of or unable to understand the circumstances of the families.

Representatives from GR-SCAN and RPS have hosted resiliency community dinners at various RPS schools. This strategy is designed to help the faculty, families, and community **R**ealize the impact trauma can have on a student's ability to be successful. School leaders are also creating safe places at schools where families can gather to discuss various trauma-related challenges or build upon their parenting skills. The schools are using a model called Circle of Parents, a national program which provides a friendly, supportive environment led by parents and other caregivers. It is a place where anyone in a parenting role can openly discuss the successes and challenges of raising children.

A Parent Realizes

Jenna White's journey into becoming an advocate for trauma-informed practices began in 2015 when she attended a special education conference hosted by Fairfax County Public Schools (FCPS). During the conference, she attended a workshop on trauma, even though she believed it did not relate to her family. It was then she **R**ealized that her son, David, was suffering from trauma.

White participated in a parenting webinar with a psychologist from Washington, DC who specializes in early childhood trauma. White hired the psychologist to do a PTSD assessment of David, and he was diagnosed with complex PTSD. The psychologist provided a one-page assessment written for teachers, coaches, and anyone involved in David's life. White explained the assessment as, "David has had these experiences, here is how he might react, here is why he might react this way, and here are some things you can do."

White began taking this information to teachers, principals, and David's IEP team. She stated, "I really felt like I had to explain everything to them. I had to teach them." She learned all she could about the impacts of trauma on children. Once she was aware of trauma, she started hearing about it more often but still felt like she was the only one coming into school and talking about PTSD. "It was hard to get the words out of my mouth, and I did not feel comfortable saying *trauma*." She explained the difficulty as a parent of explaining to teachers and principals why their discipline systems, point charts, and other classroom management systems were not going to work with her child and others impacted by trauma. "Why do I have to be the one breaking the news to school personnel that this is a thing, and why do I have to explain it to them? Why do I have to provide the solutions? Obviously, I want to be part, but I felt like a lot was falling on me as a parent."

White said she knew she had to keep talking about trauma. In the Spring of 2018, White attended a trauma workshop hosted by the Parent Resource Center for FCPS and discovered there were actions taking place in the schools and community. At this workshop, White became aware of the Trauma-Informed Community Network (TICN) in Fairfax County, a powerful coalition where she met others who were advocating for trauma-awareness.

A Superintendent Realizes

Loudoun County Public Schools (LCPS) came to trauma-awareness through their long-term commitment to Positive Behavioral Interventions and Supports (PBIS). In 2007, PBIS was initiated in a few schools and developed to scale by 2012. The impetus at the time was not framed as trauma-related, but as a way to prevent violence and reduce disciplinary referrals and exclusionary discipline. According to *John Lody*, director of diagnostic and prevention services, Department of Pupil Services (DPS), "Our charge was to improve school climate, teach prosocial behaviors, and increase the chance that all kids will be engaged in the learning process."

In 2012, the school board Realized that while PBIS had helped reduce overall exclusionary discipline, there were still issues to address. Those who were suspended were disproportionately Black or SWD. According to

Lody, a discipline task force was formed. "We started to look behind the curtain and began to see disparate outcomes for students of color and students of disability." At that time, members of DPS became more focused on equity outcomes and supports for students with greater behavioral needs.

By the time *Eric Williams* became superintendent in 2014, the division had systemic supports in place with PBIS, a multi-tiered system of supports (MTSS), and restorative practices, resulting in a reduction in disproportionality of out-of-school suspensions among Black students and SWD. Williams maintained focus on these successful programs, while another challenge required him to specifically focus the division on trauma-awareness. In 2014, suicide surpassed cancer as the second leading cause of death among teens in the US (Tuttle, 2017). On October 15, 2014, Woodgrove High School student Ryan Bartel, a suburban middle-class White student, took his own life. In 2015, another LCPS student died by suicide. In 2016, the division mourned five additional teen suicides, and in 2017 three more (Edmunds & Heymann, 2017). Facing a tragic mental health crisis in the community, Williams won urgent school board approval in 2017 for additional staff positions to create a larger mental health framework. According to the *Loudoun County Times Mirror* (2017), LCPS added eight social workers, eight school counselors, five psychologists and two student assistance specialists. Williams said the intention was "to build on existing efforts to promote mental wellness and resiliency, increase early detection, provide social and emotional support, and encourage help-seeking behavior and access to mental health treatment" (Edmunds & Heymann, 2017, para. 63). The division partnered with the Ryan Bartel Foundation, started in 2014 by the parents of Ryan Bartel. The Ryan Bartel Foundation has served as a community coalition to bolster the following:

> **AWARENESS** about the causes behind this growing, senseless epidemic of youth suicide through programs and outreach among our schools and communities.

> **EDUCATIONAL PROGRAMS** on developing coping skills during the ups and downs of life, providing acceptance of everyone, while encouraging youth to develop confidence and self-esteem.

> **ACTIVITIES** inspired by our youth who are struggling. We aim to empower them to create their own programs that stimulate their interests and help others who have similar issues, giving them a feeling of normalcy, purpose, strength and renewed interest in life.

> (Ryan Bartel Foundation, 2019, para. 7–9)

Educational Experts Coach Realization

John Richardson-Lauve, director of mental health, ChildSavers, states he has respect for focusing on trauma-awareness because "it plants a seed." Richardson-Lauve added, "I spend more time on the brain and understanding the experience of trauma. If I don't get you bought into the problem, I'm not going to get you to be a part of the solution." He structures his professional development around Substance Abuse and Mental Health Services (SAMSHA)'s Four **R**s and emphasizes the importance of resilience. The majority of the professional development Richardson-Lauve provides is in response to division or school leadership requests for a broad trauma and resilience overview. "When we deliver professional development to division leadership and principals, that's when the magic happens. We can get buy-in and then they can go and be champions in their schools."

As an external support with no exposure to education coursework, *Allison Sampson-Jackson*, CEO, Integration Solutions Inc., has learned a lot about how schools function and the role of leadership. Sampson-Jackson **R**ealized the critical role of the building level principal in the successful implementation of trauma-responsive practices. In an effort to increase her skills to coach school leaders, she became a certified facilitator of Brene Brown's *Dare to Lead* Model in January 2019.

> What I'm finding in schools, is this takes a huge level of courage because at the moment even though there's legislation coming down saying we want this, there are no metrics that actually give educational systems credit for investing in [trauma-responsive] practices. [Trauma-responsive] practices are a priority until April and May when school leaders completely panic and drop everything because of state assessments. You have to have a principal or a superintendent [who is dedicated] to say, "I know this is important and I know that the state systems will catch up."

Currently, the emphasis on standardized assessments as the primary accountability measure makes it challenging for educators to shift the focus to SEL, self-regulation, and restorative practices. Sampson-Jackson believes leaders have to be confident the investment in trauma-responsive practices will pay off because it will support academic success. "Initially I was doing training for all different kinds of schools and divisions around ACEs and learning how ACEs affect the brain and the limbic system, but I quickly **R**ealized we needed a visual to represent how [**R**esponding to] trauma can impact learning in schools." Figure 4.2 is Sampson-Jackson's representation of foundations needed to positively impact student achievement.

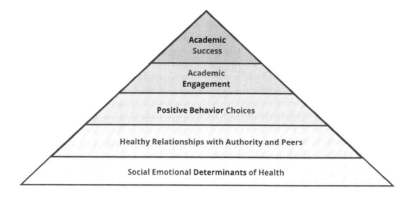

Figure 4.2 Hierarchy of the Development of Students' Skills (A. Sampson-Jackson, personal communication, 2018)

Jessica Hawthorne, director of programs, Virginia Center for Inclusive Communities (VCIC), described VCIC's mission simply as "success through inclusion." She defined inclusion as "accepting, respecting and valuing diversity through belonging, achieving, and contributing." She said she **R**ealized identifying differences can be controversial and difficult to talk about, "but in order to have that inclusion, we have to acknowledge difference, and we have to then work with it and leverage it toward equity." In other words, VCIC staff members do not see difference as a deficit but as an opportunity to meet the needs of the groups with whom they work "on all issues, for all ages, all across Virginia." Through customized programming and intensive conversations, VCIC staff members do everything from hour-long professional development sessions for business leaders to one-day forums for teachers and intensive week-long retreats for teens.

Hawthorne noted that the importance of **R**ealizing childhood trauma is a serious inequity some students bring with them to school. Although VCIC trainers do not consider themselves trauma-informed experts, Hawthorne clarified, "We do want people to **R**ealize that some of these things are probably coming out of trauma or traumatic events that may currently be happening to students or that may have already happened and are [being carried] forward." As a result, ACEs and related trauma are factors VCIC staff members include in their programming. Being aware of childhood trauma allows educators to better respond when they see it, and this creates a sense of belonging. Hawthorne explained *belonging* is a critical factor to building student resilience in the classroom. "Students need to know they are safe, valued, learning, have some power, and can make mistakes without losing their dignity."

Resources to Realize

We selected the resources below based on research and feedback from practitioners. The list is not exhaustive, rather a starting point for educators interested in developing trauma-awareness in their schools to *create a sense of urgency* and *build a guiding coalition*.

Title	Type	Description	QR Code/Link	Link
ACEs Primer	VIDEO	Brief overview of the original ACEs study.		https://tiresources.pub/1
Resilience Documentary	VIDEO	Documentary about the science behind ACEs and how trauma can impact learning.		https://tiresources.pub/2
Paper Tigers Documentary	VIDEO	Documentary about a high school's journey to becoming trauma-responsive.		https://tiresources.pub/3
Love Them First	VIDEO	Documentary about an urban elementary school's path to success.		https://tiresources.pub/4
Dr. Nadine Burke Harris	VIDEO	A pediatrician's story of how she came to understand how childhood trauma effects health across a lifetime.		https://tiresources.pub/5
Flip Your Lid	VIDEO	Dr. Daniel Siegel explains his hand model used to demonstrate how trauma can impact decision making		https://tiresources.pub/6
A Call to Connection	VIDEO	Dr. Allison Sampson-Jackson explains the importance of relationships to build resilience.		https://tiresources.pub/7
Learning Brain vs. Survival Brain	VIDEO	Understand how students function in a learning brain versus a survival brain.		https://tiresources.pub/8
Fall-Hamilton Elementary	VIDEO	Highlights whole school strategies, self-care for teachers, and an intervention for students.		https://tiresources.pub/9
Culture of Compassion	VIDEO	Story about how a diverse elementary school became trauma-responsive by partnering with families.		https://tiresources.pub/10

Figure 4.3 Resources to Realize

Title	Type	Description	QR Code/Link	Link
Brain Architecture Game	ACTIVITY	Hour and a half activity designed for small groups to demonstrate how ACEs can impact brain development.		https://tiresources.pub/11
ACEs Connection	WEBSITE	An online community designed to inform professionals. Join and receive regular emails with resources.		https://tiresources.pub/12
A System Framework	REFERENCE DOCUMENT	The National Child Traumatic Stress Network (NCTSN) outlines core areas of trauma-responsive schools.		https://tiresources.pub/13
Understanding Child Trauma	REFERENCE DOCUMENT	A three-page infographic about childhood trauma developed by the NCTSN and the Substance Abuse and Mental Health Services Administration (SAMHSA).		https://tiresources.pub/14
Helping Traumatized Children Learn	REFERENCE DOCUMENT	Comprehensive resources created by the Trauma and Learning Policy Initiative to support educators with implementing trauma-informed practices.		https://tiresources.pub/15
The Heart of Teaching and Learning	REFERENCE DOCUMENT	Highlights how trauma can impact learning. Created by the Compassionate Schools Initiative in Washington.		https://tiresources.pub/16
Midwest PBIS Network	WEBSITE	Comprehensive resources to integrate PBIS and mental health supports. See "Mental Health Integration (ISF)".		https://tiresources.pub/17
Center for Parent Information	WEBSITE	A resource to share with families to assist with understanding and supporting students impacted by trauma.		https://tiresources.pub/18
Circle of Parents	WEBSITE	A nonprofit organization offering resources for families and a safe place to engage in collaborative problem solving about parenting.		https://tiresources.pub/21

Figure 4.3 Continued

References

Edmunds, C., & Heymann, A. (2017, July 15). With student suicides on the rise in Loudoun County, parents say school leaders lack compassion. *Loudoun Times Mirror*. Retrieved from https://www.loudountimes.com/news/with-student-sui cides-on-the-rise-in-loudoun-county-parents/articlea0b33e2f-1cf1-5ccc-8ee6-4238d7401eac.html.

Gorski, P. C. (2018). *Reaching and teaching students in poverty: Strategies for erasing the opportunity gap*, 2nd ed. New York: Teachers' College Press.

Greater Richmond Stop Child Abuse Now (GR-SCAN). (2019). *The Circle Preschool Program*. Retrieved from http://grscan.com/programs/the-circle-pr eschool-program/

Kotter, J. P. (2012). *Leading change*. Boston, MA: Harvard Business School Press.

Lumpkin, A. (2008). Three keys to success for principals (and their teachers). *Kappa Delta Pi Record*, *45*(1), 22–25.

Missouri Department of Mental Health and Partners. (2014). *Missouri model: A developmental framework for trauma informed approaches*. Retrieved from https://dmh.mo.gov/trauma/MO%20Model%20Working%20Document%20febr uary%202015.pdf.

Ryan Bartel Foundation (2019). Our story. Retrieved from https://www.ryanbart elfoundation.org/our-story.

Substance Abuse and Mental Health Services Administration. (2014). *Guiding principles of trauma-informed care*. *22*(2). Retrieved from https://www.samhsa .gov/samhsaNewsLetter/Volume_22_Number_2/trauma_tip/guiding_principles .html.

Tuttle, C. (2017, June 2). Curbing teen suicide in Loudoun County. *The Woodgrove Outlander*. Retrieved from https://www.thewoodgroveoutlander.com/features /2017/06/02/curbing-teen-suicide-loudoun-county/.

5 Recognize

Acknowledging Trauma and Resilience

Once faculty and staff have an awareness of trauma and resilience, they are ready to become *trauma-sensitive*. According to the Missouri Model, trauma-sensitive organizations have begun to: (1) explore the principles of trauma-informed care within their environment and daily work; (2) build consensus around the principles; (3) consider the implications of adopting the principles within the organization; and (4) prepare for change (Missouri Department of Mental Health and Partners, 2014, p. 3). In this chapter, we follow this sequence to **R**ecognize trauma in students and our ability to teach them resilience. We also discuss how to *form and communicate a strategic vision* for doing so (Kotter, 2012).

Figure 5.1 Discipline Reform Model: RECOGNIZE Source: (Kotter, 2012; Missouri Department of Mental Health and Partners, 2014; Substance Abuse and Mental Health Services Administration, 2014)

Step One: Explore the Principles of Trauma-Informed Care

The principles of trauma-informed care (TIC)—safety, choice and control, collaboration, trustworthiness, and empowerment—are present to varying degrees in every school or school division. They are synonymous with having a culture of *respect*. We often tell children that giving others respect earns respect. The same rule applies for teachers and administrators earning respect from students. The principles of TIC are measures for how educators should treat every individual child and especially those who are demonstrating signs of trauma. Being trauma-sensitive means acknowledging childhood trauma in real time and adhering to the principles of TIC.

Safety

The perception of *safety* involves both physical and emotional security. While a school or classroom may be physically safe, it may feel emotionally unsafe to students experiencing trauma. Perception is reality until we change it. All members of a school community are more likely to perceive the school as a safe place when common areas are welcoming, clean, and in good repair. The manner in which all students, staff, and visitors are greeted in the front office, on school buses, and in classrooms is also critical. Modeling expectations for how adults and students interact sets an example of inclusivity within and outside of the classroom. When schools make emotional security a priority, awareness, tolerance, understanding, and empathy increase. Cultural stereotypes and implicit biases begin to be overcome.

The perception of safety in a school also relates to discipline and a shared understanding of rules and consequences. All community members should understand the need for ensuring safety. Clearly communicating and teaching the reasons for rules and expectations develops a sense of shared responsibility. When rules are broken, students must understand the real or potential impact of their actions on others. Accepting responsibility and learning from mistakes make repeated offenses less likely. Students are more likely to accept responsibility for their actions when they do not feel ostracized by a teacher or administrator.

Choice and Control

Opportunities for redemption or reconciliation provide students with a measure of *choice and control*. Restorative practices and restorative justice are responsive ways in which students can be personally invested to be a part of a solution (see Chapter 6: **R**espond). Including students in developing school or classroom rules is a proactive way to help them **R**ecognize their individual and collective responsibility to maintain safety and orderliness. Then when students do break rules, they will more readily understand the impact of an action and its consequences. Then students will be more invested in finding ways to make wrongs right.

Collaboration

All teachers can generate class rules of mutual respect and responsibility through a facilitative process of *collaboration* with their students. Collaboration gives students a sense of autonomy. Teachers can provide age-appropriate opportunities discussing school rules, expectations, and curriculum. Project-based learning, team building activities, and peer mediation give opportunities for peer support and problem solving. Collaboration provides students with a choice in how to work together and a process of building trust in one another.

Trustworthiness

Establishing *trustworthiness* in students requires consistency, clear expectations, transparency, honesty, open communication, inclusion, and reciprocity. If students see adults as trustworthy they will work harder to gain (or regain) trustworthiness themselves. Trustworthiness develops a positive self-image in students and translates confidence into empowerment.

Empowerment

Empowerment occurs when teachers and administrators **R**ecognize each student's contributions as unique and valuable, and they invest in them. Being validating and affirming in all interactions makes students work harder and hold higher expectations for themselves. Empowerment gives students the skills they need to be resilient and to lead others to do the same.

Step Two: Build Consensus Around the Principles

Building consensus around the principles of TIC helps to create a trauma-sensitive staff that is able **R**ecognize the signs and symptoms of trauma and the importance of building resilience. A trauma-sensitive staff motivates an intentional growth process for every student academically, socially, emotionally, and behaviorally.

Recognizing the Signs and Symptoms of Trauma

To **R**ecognize trauma, it is important to acknowledge two fundamental truths: (1) all behavior communicates needs; and (2) needs determine brain states. These truths are summed up by Alan E. Beck's adage about teaching: "You can't do the Bloom stuff until you take care of the Maslow stuff" (Harris & Petaccio, 2017), or more colloquially, "You gotta Maslow before you can Bloom." In other words, learning can take place only after the basic hierarchy of needs is met. Figure 5.2 illustrates Maslow's Hierarchy of Needs as foundational to Bloom's Taxonomy (Guditas, 2013).

Understanding Brain States. Needs dictate brain states, and brain states determine behavior. Humans have three basic brain states: Survival (Downstairs Brain), Emotional (Big Feelings), and Executive (Upstairs Brain) (Bailey, 2018; Payne, 2018; Siegel, 2010; Wood, 2018). See Figure 5.3. The Downstairs Brain processes immediate need and dictates flight, fight, or freeze responses to danger. Big Feelings processes emotion. The Upstairs brain is where logical, executive functioning and learning take place and where emotion is regulated. When the Upstairs Brain is over-stimulated and stops being able to regulate emotion, students may "flip their lids" and their Downstairs Brain takes over (Payne, 2018). When students are in their Downstairs Brain, they are communicating the need for safety. Without intervention, behavior follows a predictable pattern of alarm, resistance, and exhaustion. To move students to their Upstairs Brain, the only place where resilience can develop, educators must first connect with

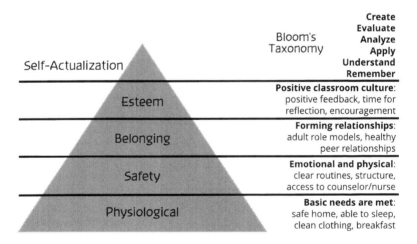

Figure 5.2 Maslow's Hierachy of School Needs Source: (Guditas, 2013)

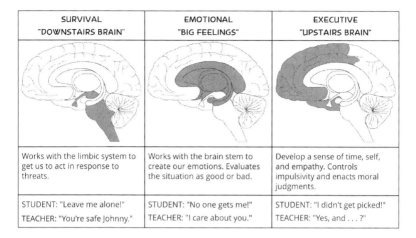

SURVIVAL "DOWNSTAIRS BRAIN"	EMOTIONAL "BIG FEELINGS"	EXECUTIVE "UPSTAIRS BRAIN"
Works with the limbic system to get us to act in response to threats.	Works with the brain stem to create our emotions. Evaluates the situation as good or bad.	Develop a sense of time, self, and empathy. Controls impulsivity and enacts moral judgments.
STUDENT: "Leave me alone!" TEACHER: "You're safe Johnny."	STUDENT: "No one gets me!" TEACHER: "I care about you."	STUDENT: "I didn't get picked!" TEACHER: "Yes, and . . . ?"

Figure 5.3 Brain states Source: (Bailey, 2018; Payne, 2018; Siegel, 2010; Wood, 2018)

students' Big Feelings and get them back to their Upstairs Brain (Siegel, 2010; Wood, 2018).

Identifying Needs-Based Behaviors. Being trauma-sensitive requires being able to identify needs-based behaviors. Children who have experienced traumatic events may have behavioral outbursts, "or their suffering may not be apparent at all" (NCTSN, 2008, p. 7). The responses to trauma are individualized and may manifest in many different ways. Students may exhibit *hyper-arousal*, demonstrated through anger, fighting, "hyperactivity," excessive talking, etc. Other students may exhibit *hypo-arousal*, such as dissociation or sleeping in class (see Figure 5.4). Behaviors related to

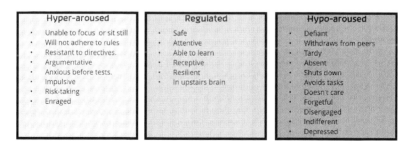

Hyper-aroused	Regulated	Hypo-aroused
• Unable to focus or sit still	• Safe	• Defiant
• Will not adhere to rules	• Attentive	• Withdraws from peers
• Resistant to directives.	• Able to learn	• Tardy
• Argumentative	• Receptive	• Absent
• Anxious before tests.	• Resilient	• Shuts down
• Impulsive	• In upstairs brain	• Avoids tasks
• Risk-taking		• Doesn't care
• Enraged		• Forgetful
		• Disengaged
		• Indifferent
		• Depressed

Figure 5.4 Behaviours Associated with Hyper-Aroused & Hypo-Aroused Children Source: (Losen, Hodson, Keith, Morrison, & Belway, 2015)

trauma may begin immediately after the trauma is experienced or may begin many years later.

Faculty and staff must work with and educate families to help children be physiologically and mentally prepared for learning in their Upstairs Brain (Wood, 2018). Educators also need to understand and share with families that the age of a student will be a factor in the student's response emotionally and behaviorally to trauma in his or her life. Examples of common behaviors in each age group include:

- Preschool – regression, separation anxiety, difficulty sleeping.
- Elementary school – distrust, headaches, stomach aches, withdrawal.
- Middle school – avoidance, emotional numbing, irritability.
- High school – aggressive behaviors, absenteeism, substance abuse (NCTSN, 2018).

See Figure 5.5 for a more comprehensive list of trauma-related behaviors across age levels.

Many students affected by trauma exhibit their feelings with overt behaviors. Typically, teachers' attention is drawn to students who cannot stay in their seats, display anger outbursts, and/or avoid tasks (NCTSN, 2008). Teachers who ask, "What happened to you?" rather than "What is wrong with you?" **R**ecognize that student behavior is another form of student communication. Some students impacted by trauma internalize their feelings and portray a facade of perfection, while anxiety, fear, and/or worry occupy their thoughts (NCTSN, 2008). Teachers must be skilled at **R**ecognizing possible signs that could indicate a student is impacted by trauma.

Although most teacher education programs include coursework in behavior management, special education teachers are uniquely qualified to assess behaviors. Special education teacher preparation programs usually include coursework to determine the function of student behavior and to develop Behavior Intervention Plans (BIPs). Pre-service special education teachers learn how to identify the setting, event, antecedents, and consequences of student behavior. Behaviors that do not align with classroom expectations may communicate a desire to avoid or get something. General education teachers may often conclude that poor student behavior is a personal affront (e.g., intentional disrespect). Completion of a Functional Behavioral Assessment (FBA) can reveal other motives, such as those shown in Figure 5.6.

We recommend completing FBAs and BIPs for general education students as needed. A special education teacher's expertise should be included to *avoid* referral to special education. It is also important to consult a trauma-informed professional, such as a school psychologist, social worker,

...preschool students.

• Separation anxiety or clinginess towards teachers or primary caregivers

• Regression in previously mastered stages of development (e.g., baby talk or bedwetting/toileting accidents)

• Lack of developmental progress (e.g., not progressing at same level as peers)

• Re-creating the traumatic event (e.g., repeatedly talking about, "playing" out, or drawing the event)

• Difficulty at naptime or bedtime (e.g., avoiding sleep, waking up, or nightmares)

• Increased somatic complaints (e.g., headaches, stomachaches, overreacting to minor bumps and bruises)

• Changes in behavior (e.g., appetite, unexplained absences, angry outbursts, decreased attention, withdrawal)

• Over- or under-reacting to physical contact, bright lighting, sudden movements, or loud sounds (e.g., bells, slamming doors, or sirens)

• Increased distress (unusually whiny, irritable, moody)

• Anxiety, fear, and worry about safety of self and others

• Worry about recurrence of the traumatic event

• New fears (e.g., fear of the dark, animals, or monsters)

• Statements and questions about death and dying

...elementary students.

• Anxiety, fear, and worry about safety of self and others (more clingy with teacher or parent)

• Worry about recurrence of violence • Increased distress (unusually whiny, irritable, moody)

• Changes in behavior:
 • Increase in activity level
 • Decreased attention and/or concentration
 • Withdrawal from others or activities
 • Angry outbursts and/or aggression
 • Absenteeism

• Distrust of others, affecting how children interact with both adults and peers

• A change in ability to interpret and respond appropriately to social cues

• Increased somatic complaints (e.g., headaches, stomachaches, overreaction to minor bumps and bruises)

• Changes in school performance

• Recreating the event (e.g., repeatedly talking about, "playing" out, or drawing the event)

• Over- or under-reacting to bells, physical contact, doors slamming, sirens, lighting, sudden movements

• Statements and questions about death and dying

• Difficulty with authority, redirection, or criticism • Re-experiencing the trauma (e.g., nightmares or disturbing memories during the day)

• Hyper-arousal (e.g., sleep disturbance, tendency to be easily startled)

• Avoidance behaviors (e.g., resisting going to places that remind them of the event)

• Emotional numbing (e.g., seeming to have no feeling about the event)

...middle school students.

• Anxiety, fear, and worry about safety of self and others

• Worry about recurrence or consequences of violence

• Changes in behavior:
 • Decreased attention and/or concentration
 • Increase in activity level
 • Change in academic performance
 • Irritability with friends, teachers, events
 • Angry outbursts and/or aggression
 • Withdrawal from others or activities
 • Absenteeism

• Increased somatic complaints (e.g., headaches, stomachaches, chest pains)

• Discomfort with feelings (such as troubling thoughts of revenge)

• Repeated discussion of event and focus on specific details of what happened

• Over- or under-reacting to bells, physical contact, doors slamming, sirens, lighting, sudden movements

• Re-experiencing the trauma (e.g., nightmares or disturbing memories during the day)

• Hyperarousal (e.g., sleep disturbance, tendency to be easily startled)

• Avoidance behaviors (e.g., resisting going to places that remind them of the event)

• Emotional numbing (e.g., seeming to have no feeling about the event)

...high school students.

• Anxiety, fear, and worry about safety of self and others

• Worry about recurrence or consequences of violence

• Changes in behavior:
 • Withdrawal from others or activities
 • Irritability with friends, teachers, events
 • Angry outbursts and/or aggression
 • Change in academic performance
 • Decreased attention and/or concentration
 • Increase in activity level
 • Absenteeism
 • Increase in impulsivity, risk-taking behavior

• Discomfort with feelings (such as troubling thoughts of revenge)

• Increased risk for substance abuse

• Discussion of events and reviewing of details

• Negative impact on issues of trust and perceptions of others

• Over- or under-reacting to bells, physical contact, doors slamming, sirens, lighting, sudden movements

• Repetitive thoughts and comments about death or dying (including suicidal thoughts, writing, art, or notebook covers about violent or morbid topics, internet searches)

• Heightened difficulty with authority, redirection, or criticism

• Re-experiencing the trauma (e.g., nightmares or disturbing memories during the day)

• Hyperarousal (e.g., sleep disturbance, tendency to be easily startled)

• Avoidance behaviors (e.g., resisting going to places that remind them of the event)

• Emotional numbing

Figure 5.5 Recognize trauma in… Source: (NCTSN, 2018, pp. 8–13)

Get/Obtain:	Protest/Escape/Avoid:
Choice	Tasks, a demand or request being made
Attention in the form of social status in a group interaction with peer(s) interaction with adults	A specific person, a group of people
Objects, including $	Objects, undesired
Internal events (e.g., brain chemical release) on some occasions in self abusive behavior	Internal events (e.g., upcoming seizure/migraine)
Make instructional material more meaningful	Lack of meaning/relevance of instructional material
Self-stimulation	Protest, a past action by a person (do not use "revenge," vengeance")
Play, fun	Protest, a lack of choice (do not use "control")
Replication of a chain of behavior	Avoidance of step one in an anticipated chain of behavior
Justice or fairness	Protest, a lack of fairness, justice (do not use "revenge," vengeance")
Sensory input	Sensory Input

Figure 5.6 Possible Functions of Behavior Source: (McIntosh & Goodman, 2016)

or behavior specialist, for assistance. Including a parent or guardian in the FBA process is important to be consistent with the principles of TIC.

Once an intervention team has completed an FBA and has a hypothesis about the function of a student's behavior, a replacement behavior should be identified. In order to support the student with the transition to the use of a new behavior, a Behavior Intervention Plan (BIP for SPED students) or a Behavior Support Plan (BSP for non-SPED students) should be monitored across settings within the school.

We recommend a simple "three hat" method. In the first hat the team identifies non-negotiable behaviors that absolutely cannot be tolerated (e.g., fighting). The second hat identifies behaviors for the student to work on and be rewarded for at school and at home with positive behavioral goals, supports, and incentives (e.g., following directions, demonstrating respect). The third hat identifies behaviors that are just not worth addressing immediately—behaviors you can forgive and avoid trying to control (e.g., standing while working).

Other designated staff, such as school counselors, can communicate with all of a student's teachers about a student's BIP/BSP and requirements for frequent progress monitoring. Data collection will indicate if the selected replacement behavior is meeting the student's needs by a decrease in discipline issues. If discipline issues do not decrease, the designated staff member should reexamine the hypothesized function of the student's behavior and bring it back to the team. An important part of any FBA is to identify student "triggers" that may set them off. An intervention team may need to Recognize that a teacher's behaviors can be such a trigger.

Identifying Triggers. Exclusionary discipline of any kind can be a trigger that worsens student behavior. Furthermore, office discipline referrals (ODRs) disproportionately affect Black students and students with disabilities (SWD) for subjective conduct violations (e.g., Defiance, Disruption, Disrespect). While the 3Ds may be manifestations of trauma, they may also be a reaction to implicit teacher bias. In a trauma-sensitive school, teachers must **R**ecognize what implicit bias is and that it may affect their own interactions with some students. They may, indeed, be provoking student behaviors themselves (Gregory & Weinstein, 2008).

Cultural competence training (see Chapter 6: **R**espond) can help to mitigate the effects of implicit bias by teaching staff to **R**ecognize their own vulnerable decision points. A vulnerable decision point is "a specific decision that is more vulnerable to effects of implicit bias" and is affected by the situation and a person's internal state (McIntosh, 2017). According to national data, most ODRs are written in the afternoon. Students may be tired or bored and acting out, or it may be that teachers are less patient later in the day (McIntosh, 2017).

Teachers need to **R**ecognize their own vulnerable decision points throughout the day and which student behaviors may trigger their negative response. Students affected by trauma need regulated adults to support them. For adults to make well-informed decisions during chaotic and ambiguous situations, a neutralizing routine must be in place (Danzinger et al., 2011). Neutralizing routines allow teachers to create enough time to reflect and **R**espond versus react to student behavior. An effective neutralizing routine is brief, has clear steps, is doable, starts with an if-then statement, and successfully interrupts the chain of events (McIntosh, 2017).

For example, a fifth grade science teacher is really excited about a photosynthesis lesson she stayed up late to prepare the night before. As class begins, one student begins mumbling under her breath and rolling her eyes. The teacher is exhausted and has already redirected this student three times that day for talking during instruction. The teacher knows it is the end of the day and her patience is running low, so she takes a deep breath and asks herself, "If I raise my voice at the student, then I am not setting a good example for how to handle frustration." This brief neutralizing routine allowed the teacher to control the situation rather than react to student behavior.

Trauma-sensitive staff **R**ecognize how their own behaviors can affect students. They consciously plan to avoid negative reactions when faced with vulnerable decision points to foster a safe and predictable learning environment. Teachers who model neutralizing routines in their classrooms **R**ecognize the importance of building resilience in themselves and their students.

Recognizing the Importance of Building Resilience

According to the United States Marine Corps, resilience is "the process of preparing for, recovering from, and adjusting to life in the face of stress, adversity, trauma, or tragedy" (US Department of the Navy, US Marine Corps, 2010, p. 13). By necessity, the Marine Corps intentionally trains soldiers for combat resilience—physically, mentally, and spiritually—to help them meet the challenges of the next mission or successfully transition to civilian life. Similarly, "the role educators play in a child's mental health cannot be overstated" (Bell, Limberg, & Robinson, 2013, p. 142). Educators must intentionally teach and support students affected by trauma to self-regulate and overcome responses of fight, flight, or freeze (Bell et al., 2013; Forbes, 2012).

All students benefit from a safe and supportive environment, strong adult connections, and the tools to learn from their mistakes (Wood, 2018). "Students must be told what to do versus merely what not to do" (Ginsburg, 2018, para. 1). Students affected by trauma require more holistic supports, and teachers, counselors, and administrators "may be the only adults present consistently enough in a child's life to distinguish trauma-related changes from the child's normal disposition" (Bell et al., 2013, p. 140). Educators have the responsibility and opportunity to foster student resilience (Bell et al., 2013).

Dr. Rob Anda, MD, MS and co-principal investigator and co-founder of the original ACEs study, describes resilience as a message of hope and healing. "I believe everyone should know this (ACE research) because some people will find transcendence in the information and distance themselves from what happened to them and see their lives in perspective" (Community Resilience Initiative, 2018, para. 1). According to Teri Barila, co-founder and CEO of the Children's Resilience Initiative in Walla Walla, Washington, "Resilience trumps ACEs" (Community Resilience Initiative, 2018, para. 1).

Lori Wood, senior director, Virginia's Region Ten Community Services Board, recommends that faculty and staff take the ACE questionnaire and a resilience questionnaire. By reflecting on the results, they will learn to Recognize ACEs in their own lives and how resilience has empowered them to overcome them (Wood, 2018). The original *ACEs Survey* and the *Devereux Adult Resilience Survey* for administrators and their staff are available to complete in Appendix B and C. School leaders should anticipate a variety of emotional responses upon completion of these assessments, and should prepare by having trauma-informed personnel present to help faculty and staff process the experience.

Another research-informed resilience questionnaire, the *Aces Too High Resilience Questionnaire*, is available online and is useful to prompt

perspective on how protective factors such as relationships with supportive adults can build resilience (White, 2017). To clinically assess and build
resilience in children, trauma-informed psychologists use research-based
resilience questionnaires, such as the Devereux Child Assessments and the
Connor-Davidson Resilience Scale, which are available for schools to pur-
chase (White, 2017).

Dr. Kenneth Ginsburg, MD, MS Ed, identifies two bottom lines of
resilience. First, "Young people live up or down to expectations we set
for them. They need adults who believe in them unconditionally and
hold them to the high expectations of being compassionate, generous,
and creative" (Ginsburg, 2018, para. 1). Second, "What we do to model
healthy resilience strategies for our children is more important than anything we say about them" (Ginsburg, 2018, para. 2). Figure 2. 3 (page 34),
Ginsburg's *Seven Cs of Resilience*, identifies the expectations a community of educators should model and teach (Ginsburg, 2018). We suggest
having administrators and staff identify and share student success stories
with each of the seven Cs.

- Which of the seven Cs have you helped to develop in your students?
- How did you do it? Give a specific example.

By sharing experiences, educators will **R**ecognize they already have what it
takes to build resilience in their students. They may also rekindle a passion
for their profession.

Asking parents to work on the seven Cs with their children is a straight-
forward way to develop resilience at home. Traditionally, schools measure
parent engagement by the number of families attending school events (e.g.,
conferences, back to school night), but school leaders and teachers need
to redefine family engagement. Families may not attend school events for
a number of reasons, including lack of transportation, work schedule conflicts, and/or childcare, but that does not mean families are not invested
in their child's education (Ginsburg, 2018). The seven Cs provide teach-
ers/administrators with an opportunity to *partner* with parents in student
discipline.

Step Three: Consider the Implications of Adopting the Principles Within the Organization

Adopting the principles of TIC within a school or division requires working
with a guiding coalition to *form and communicate a strategic vision* (Kotter,
2012). A strategic vision clarifies "how the future will be different from the
past" and how initiatives are "linked directly to the vision" (Kotter, 2019).

The Role of the Principal

Principals cannot control their students' experiences outside of school; however, they can focus on creating an environment within their schools which fosters resilience. An effective principal must personally understand and develop a school culture which **R**ecognizes the impact of trauma on student learning. When the principal believes in the transformative power of adopting trauma-responsive practices, he/she becomes a much more influential change agent with the guiding coalition, faculty, support staff, families, students, and community stakeholders.

Principals who are invested in transforming a school's culture need to integrate trauma-responsive practices into their vision and with existing school and division structures. Trauma-responsive practices should not be viewed as another separate, unrelated initiative that may be abandoned. Instead, staff should feel empowered by training they receive and view it as a means to improve student outcomes. A principal who is passionate, well-informed, willing to take risks, transparent, empathetic, supportive, and con-gratulatory can energize buy-in and a paradigm-shift to trauma-sensitivity.

Principals should also prioritize teacher self-care. Trauma-sensitive teachers who build strong trusting relationships with students are often exposed to secondary trauma. "Secondary trauma is the emotional duress that results when an individual hears about the first-hand trauma experiences of another" (National Child Traumatic Stress Network (NCTSN), Schools Committee, 2017, para. 1). Recent research attributes teacher burnout to personality traits, role incompatibility, and the high numbers of students with significant behavior and academic needs in their classrooms (Lee, Griffin, & Keels, 2018). One way school principals can prioritize self-care is to allocate time for teachers to develop self-care plans with one another. Having "accountability partners" builds a support system among faculty/staff.

Forming a Strategic Vision

To develop a strategic vision of discipline reform, the principal and guiding coalition must first identify school or division-specific aspirations around each of the five principles of TIC. Consider the following together:

- What changes do you want to achieve together with your community to develop restorative versus punitive student discipline?
- How do these changes align with the five Principles of Trauma-Informed Care?
  - What aspects of *safety* should guide your school discipline?

- What aspects of *choice and control* should guide your school discipline?
- What aspects of *collaboration* should guide your school discipline?
- What aspects of *trustworthiness* should guide your school discipline?
- What aspects of *empowerment* should guide your school discipline?

After discussing each, write them as five individual vision statements using the Strategic Vision Builder (Appendix D). For example, *Johnson Elementary will promote physical and emotional safety among students, parents, faculty, staff, administration, volunteers, and the community*. The guiding coalition can then select trauma-responsive practices (missions) from Chapter 6 (**R**espond) that will best support these vision statements. Staffing, support, and a timeline of implementation to systematize these practices can be based on models provided in Chapter 7 (**R**esist).

Communicating a Strategic Vision

Once developed, the guiding coalition should communicate your strategic vision to all stakeholders, including teachers, staff, students, parents, and the community. The vision should be easy to explain and understand. Communication of the vision needs to be ongoing and frequent with opportunities for stakeholders to ask questions about implementation and measures of success. When communicating a vision to their stakeholders, the leaders we interviewed shared the following lessons learned:

- It is essential to communicate the prevalence of trauma in every school and every demographic.
- Have a faculty-first focus—share the vision with the faculty before the community.
- Be willing to have courageous conversations regarding cultural competence and implicit bias.
- Within a division, use guidance documents to help ensure all schools within a school system are consistent.
- Do not mandate others to follow the vision—inspire them.
- Utilize community organizations such as the PTA or a Trauma Informed Community Network (TICN) to also provide a means of communicating the vision to the community.
- Being trauma-sensitive means being able to **R**ecognize both trauma and resilience.

Step Four: Prepare for Change

On their journeys to become trauma-sensitive, the school leaders we interviewed maintained trust and transparency while forming and communicating their strategic visions. They all **R**ecognized that trauma is far more prevalent in their schools than they originally understood or anticipated, and that trauma-sensitivity was a clear prerequisite to building capacity for trauma-responsiveness. As Principal Joshua Cole **R**ecognized, "Programs do not improve school culture, people do." The stories below illustrate how individual school communities developed a vision and trauma-responsive strategies to support it. Chapter 6, **R**espond, describes these strategies in detail.

Hopewell High School Recognizes

After watching the movies *Resilience* and *Paper Tigers*, Principal *Stephanie Poe*'s teachers at Hopewell High School, Hopewell City Schools, determined their ACE scores. Anonymously, 78 of 85 teachers and four administrators submitted them to her through a Google form. Poe then created a bar graph to share the faculty's overall ACE profile. Together they discussed how their own ACEs may affect their expectations of and responses to student behavior. Teachers with low ACE scores **R**ecognized how difficult it could be to understand why some students were behaving as they were. Teachers with high ACE scores **R**ecognized how their experiences help them to better understand their students' needs.

The administrative team became trauma-sensitive by learning more about their students through questions and observations, and using that information during weekly administrator meetings. Instead of looking at a specific behavior as an isolated event, they worked to **R**ecognize needs that the behavior communicated. Then they identified how they could work with the student differently. "High-flyers" in the office, often referred for defiance and disrespect, required them to identify behaviors possibly related to trauma and seek orderly alternatives to suspending them.

Poe sought additional training for her administrative team to conduct behavior assessments on any student having difficulty following school rules. They began using an ABCY protocol:

- What is the *Antecedent* to the behavior?
- What is the actual *Behavior*?
- What are the positive or negative *Consequences* of the behavior to others?
- *WhY* is the student exhibiting the behavior?

The answers to these questions were explored together with the students and sometimes with parents. "While this process takes a significant amount of time and knowledge of the student," said Poe, "we are finding success in reducing recidivism. Students are understanding their own behaviors and taking more ownership of their actions."

Ecoff Elementary School Recognizes

Joshua Cole, principal, Ecoff Elementary, Chesterfield County Public Schools (CCPS), formed a trauma leadership team and recruited faculty members who were interested in learning more about becoming a trauma-responsive school. The group was tasked with identifying needs and challenges at the school and then researching potential strategies or programs to address those needs while supporting student growth.

The committee worked together to implement and analyze a needs assessment (which Cole called an "equity audit") to evaluate the overall effectiveness of the school's current programs. The group agreed it was important to focus on the "whole child" with an emphasis on the five competencies from the Collaborative for Academic, Social, and Emotional Learning (CASEL): *self-awareness*, *self-control*, *social awareness*, *responsible decision-making*, and *relationship skills* (Collaborative for Academic, Social, and Emotional Learning, 2018).

Cole cited *Courageous Conversations About Race* by Glenn Singleton as particularly impactful in helping him communicate effectively with teachers. He emphasized the value of helping people have courageous conversations. "Get comfortable feeling uncomfortable," is a slogan Cole used to encourage his teachers to take risks, engage in challenging conversations, "and embrace the fact we are learning new strategies." He wanted everyone to be willing and eager to discuss strategies and ideas with one another.

The professional development organized by Cole's team helped teachers to better **R**ecognize the signs of student behavior resulting from trauma in a student's life. *Bridget Manuel*, third grade teacher, and *Natalie White*, special education teacher, each said they learned that writing a referral or having a student removed from class as a result of inappropriate behavior did not help the student to grow or develop. *Kelsey Taylor*, fifth grade teacher, explained how the focus of the teachers shifted from identifying inappropriate student behaviors and administering discipline to analyzing behaviors and determining what supports the student might need to be successful.

Henrico County Public Schools (HCPS) Recognizes

Nyah Hamlett, assistant superintendent for instructional support, Henrico County Public Schools (HCPS), coordinates intensive supports for the 2% of students county-wide who have two or more out-of-school suspensions. She said these students are disproportionately Black students or students with disabilities (SWD).

> We started looking where geographically in Henrico students were being suspended. That is what led us to strategically place our preventive programs in areas in our county or in specific schools where there was a triangulation of poverty, low student performance, and disproportionate discipline rates.

In 2017–2018, the majority of students with three or more out-of-school suspensions were Black and attended schools with greater than 75% Free and Reduced Lunch rate. According to Hamlett, HCPS provided these schools with professional development on alternatives to exclusionary discipline and cultural proficiency training. The Office of Equity and Diversity partnered with the Virginia Center for Inclusive Communities (VCIC) in this effort. Hamlett added:

> We are making sure that we move in a direction where [cultural proficiency training] is a requirement and not just a 'nice to have training' mentality. It should also be ongoing and focus on more than just Black and White, rich and poor. We have to look at, for example, discipline rights of students with disabilities or discipline rights of Black males or other groups. When you see students who tend to be suspended two or more times, there's usually some type of cultural mismatch between the instructors and the students, sometimes even in some of our East End schools that have higher rates of students of color and their teachers and administrators are also people of color.

Recognizing the need to focus on both trauma and implicit bias, Hamlett outlined a vision for HCPS to be a restorative practices school division with training and supports in all 72 schools.

William Noel, Sr., director of student support and disciplinary review, similarly sees cultural proficiency and restorative practices as important means for teachers to develop a trauma-sensitive lens.

> We all know that schools are designed to educate, but it's so much more that we have to do. We have to educate the whole child. We have to

touch a child's brain and a child's heart. So much of what our children go through, long before they get to us, has taken root in their lives, and if they have had traumatic upbringings it's going to come to school with them. But if you don't know your student, all you see is a student coming in putting his head down and you're thinking, "Don't be lazy. Pay attention." As a teacher, you want the child to learn the reasons for the War of 1812, but what if the child came from a home where maybe he had a fight with his mom or dad that morning? Maybe the electricity is off, maybe the water's off. Maybe they don't have anything to eat. Maslow's hierarchy of needs starts with safety, and that's where that child's mind is. If you don't know that, then we're going to have an issue. You're going to say something to the child and the child is going to have an outburst. But if you know what's going on maybe you will be looking more delicately in how you approach it. You still approach it, you stay focused, but you just keep in mind where the child might be before you say something.

A Suburban School Division Recognizes

John Lody, director of diagnostic and prevention services, Loudoun County Public Schools (LCPS), noted implementation of Positive Behavior Intervention and Supports (PBIS) took approximately the same time—three to five years—as it takes for all new initiatives to be systematized in LCPS. Systematization means fidelity of implementation in all 92 schools. To get there, Lody described a bottom-up versus top-down vision of change. "We almost never use the word mandate. We use the word inspire." Starting with a volunteer pilot school or even a grade level that is "primed for success," LCPS develops peer-to-peer momentum; "and once we get a school that's at a high level of implementation, we often lean on those principals and administrators to help us market and make a case for other schools to do it." Lody also noted that the nature of psychologists' and social workers' jobs have dramatically changed by supporting kids "quickly and early" with evidence-based approaches.

Lisa Fillipovich, coordinator of PBIS, explained that one of the barriers to teacher buy-in is lack of preparedness to handle behaviors and social concerns. "Most teacher education programs don't spend a lot of time on behavior management or mental health. I think teachers may be resistant to new things because they are unsure. But we provide them with so much professional development in this area that once they see the support and learn those skills, they become more willing."

Jennifer Wall, licensed professional counselor and supervisor of student assistance specialists, saw the need to even further expand the lens through which teachers approach behavior, learning, and mental health needs of all students. Wall contracted training by the International Institute of Restorative Practices (IIRP) in social-emotional learning (SEL), restorative language, circles, and conferencing. The initiative started with four IIRP certified trainers and increased capacity with turn-around training of additional staff, including administrators, counselors, and teachers for SEL in the classroom. In 2015, LCPS received a grant from the Department of Juvenile Justice to extend training to probation officers and school resource officers. Wall further described the benefit teachers see in the classroom. "With restorative circles, once teachers realize how simple it is to apply, the feedback is that they start hearing from kids they haven't heard from the whole year. They are now actually having the opportunity to express their concerns in the classroom and be heard."

According to Wall, teachers are using the meetings daily in every LCPS school, K-12, including the juvenile detention center. Faculty have also seen the benefits of support circles for themselves when student behaviors have resulted in secondary trauma. Restorative practices are part of the LCPS discipline handbook and given to administrators as an option to consider before alternative forms of discipline are explored.

The division also has a vision for suicide prevention. In addition to increased staffing, LCPS adopted a suicide screening tool, *The Columbia Suicide Severity Rating Scale*, and expanded another instructional program, *Signs of Suicide (SOS)*, for all middle and high school students. *Sources of Strength*, a third initiative, is a recent LCPS venture in SEL. Lody noted the research behind *Sources of Strength* is around suicide prevention and anti-bullying, but Lody noted, "It has a more expansive scope than just suicide prevention—it's about wellness." Wellness, Lody explained, includes being able to cope with stress, adversity, and the daily rigors of life. "It got us thinking about what we could do systematically across schools to support student resiliency and build protective factors."

Sources of Strength is listed on the National Best Practices Registry by the Suicide Prevention Resource Center (SPRC), the American Foundation for Suicide Prevention (AFSP), and SAMHSA's National Registry of Evidence-based Programs and Practices (NREPP). Wall described the training process.

> In the first year of implementation, 2017–2018, we trained our 45 Department of Pupil Services staff, which include psychologists, social workers, and student assistant specialists. From that group we identified six trainers to become certified to help with the initial push. In the first year, we had 12 schools take on the program—10 high schools and 2 middle schools—and we now have 12 trainers with 20

schools. We continue to push and monitor it from the administrative level.

Twelve of the 15 LCPS high schools continue to use *Sources of Strength*, with a plan for integrating the approach in all high schools and middle schools. Loudoun County Public Schools has most recently identified a need to investigate more structured and developmentally appropriate SEL programs at the elementary level. Superintendent *Eric Williams* explained:

> Our next steps, in terms of SEL, are logical for a number of reasons, including the fact that we are kind of working backwards from the point of crisis of the high school to middle school and elementary school in terms of intervention and prevention. The ultimate goal is for all LCPS students, K-12, to have social and emotional wellness programs that are developmentally appropriate, build on one another, and provide students with personal tools for resilience.

Richmond Public Schools (RPS) Recognizes

Ram Bhagat, manager of school culture and climate strategy, Richmond Public Schools (RPS), stressed the importance of collective vision building. "There has to be a transition and [trauma-responsive practices] must be centered around the idea that we are a community and we must create a climate and culture where everyone is involved in taking care of everyone." He emphasized the pitfalls of not developing a collective vision. "Part of the danger of the TI (trauma-informed) movement is a lack of cohesive understanding of what TI really means and the misuse of trauma in terms of labeling, grouping, and [causing students to] still feel like they are traumatized. [We are also making comments such as] 'Those kids are traumatized, that's why they are acting like this' but not looking at the whole, [and not ensuring] enough emphasis on self-care for the teachers."

Bhagat noted that hollow implementation is often the case for restorative justice/restorative practice and circles. "They tend to be top down, where it is decided every teacher is going to do a circle every week and administrators are going to come in and check." Bhagat stressed the need for a mindset shift first. "We are designed for connections, and for students especially it is all about connections, reconnections, and feeling valued."

Margo Buchanan, resiliency project coordinator for RPS and trauma-informed child and family therapist, GR-SCAN, identified the fundamental need to provide students with a safe place to learn as one of the top priorities of a vision for change. She emphasized the importance of faculty and staff clearly understanding that students will struggle greatly to achieve when their basic need of feeling safe is not met. Simultaneously, Buchanan also acknowledged the profound challenge school administrators and teachers face when presented with an unattainable number of goals and expectations each year. For example, Buchanan shared that stakeholders, primarily teachers, will struggle with meeting curriculum expectations for a diverse group of learners while also providing the necessary trauma-responsive support. Annually, schools must meet various accreditation expectations and learning targets to be considered successful, and these expectations are often measured by a predetermined score on a state assessment. "The same score is required for all schools regardless of extenuating factors such as trauma." Buchanan advocated for patience over pressure. "Implementing trauma-responsive practices and supports must be done as a process versus a one and done approach."

Circle Preschool Program Recognizes

Denise Powers, lead early childhood specialist, Circle Preschool Program, GR-SCAN, has a vision for more early childhood programs to be focused on social and emotional support instead of strictly academics. "Often students from [other programs] know their letters and numbers, but lack regulation skills due to a lack of support." She believes change must begin with teachers **R**ecognizing trauma in their students.

> Educators need to look for the student who is dysregulated. We should also be aware of students who are dysregulated and dissociating or shutting down because these students often get overlooked. Preschoolers who respond by shutting down are often more difficult to identify and help. [They] will respond by needing to constantly use the restroom, becoming chronically ill, and [displaying] other avoidance behaviors. These chronic behaviors are also systemic. The students are [actually] having sensations that they are having headaches and need to use the restroom.

Powers elaborated on the need for teachers to have time built into their schedules to help students self-regulate. "Schedules are so tight, and there is so much pressure on administrators, teachers, and students to keep moving, keep going regardless of what is going on. That climate is detrimental to a child who has endured trauma because it triggers every red flag that something is wrong. [The teacher needs] five minutes with the child while sending the other students to another class to say, 'Hey, that was really hard. Let's take a minute, let's journal, let's draw, let's talk' and communicate to the child that you like the kid, but you do not like the attitude or behavior." Powers's vision was clear with respect to teachers becoming trauma-sensitive. Their purpose is not to have sympathy but to develop empathy, and then to act on it.

Virginia Center for Inclusive Communities (VCIC) Helps Schools to Recognize

Jessica Hawthorne, director of programs, VCIC, believes individuals must first take stock of their personal identity dimensions to understand others. "How do you identify? How are you affected by the messages you got in school and how are those related?" To answer these questions, VCIC trainers help teachers see how their identity dimensions impact the way they view themselves and the lenses through which they view and respond to conflicts with their students. Identity dimensions include, for example, family structure, career, religion, income, or marriage status.

Hawthorne was careful to disassociate interpersonal conflict from racism, defining racism as "prejudice plus power." Interpersonal conflict "may have layers of race," but exploring it directly points educators in the direction of cultural proficiency versus power." Hawthorne prefers the term "cultural proficiency" to suggest a more expansive understanding of difference and a purpose for pursuing it. "It is an understanding of my own identity and how that plays into things, and then looking at working toward inclusion and working toward equity with others." Whereas cultural competence is an understanding of differences and recognizing that even within culture there are many nuances, cultural proficiency "is knowing what questions to ask in order to inform responses."

To make cultural proficiency a dynamic process of change, Hawthorne emphasized the importance of teachers having an intentional growth mindset. Before and after training, she has teachers evaluate their individual level of cultural proficiency, as well as their school's level of cultural proficiency. The process creates buy-in to the work they must do to facilitate change within the organization.

ChildSavers Helps Schools to Recognize

John Richardson-Lauve, director of mental health, ChildSavers, is focused on helping educators Recognize that trauma-responsive practices cannot be implemented with a "check box approach."

> It's about relationships. It's about finding ways to build self-regulation skills. [If you have] students with a giant social-emotional deficit or students who have experienced trauma, then they are not going to be able to effectively learn. Their learning brain is offline, and we have to work on getting that learning brain online. That's not about being a

social worker or a therapist. That's about being a good teacher building relationships, helping kids feel known, helping kids build resilience and self-regulation skills.

In Heather Forbes's book, *Help for Billy*, she posits that 90% of school behavior problems are just about regulation. After teachers understand the brain science behind ACEs and resilience, as well as the impact on behavior and learning, Richardson-Lauve transitions to self-care. Self-care includes, "dealing with compassion fatigue, burnout, vicarious trauma, secondary trauma, and finding functional ways to honor teachers' experiences to help people develop strategies for both self-care and organizational/employee care."

Richardson-Lauve explained how deliberate questioning can support administrators working to move from **R**ealizing the impact of trauma as an issue to **R**ecognizing the need for reform. "When I meet with administrators, my big tag lines are, 'How many of you know kids who have been suspended from school?' Almost everyone's hand goes up. Then I ask, 'How many of you know somebody who's come back from a suspension with better behavior?'" In Richardson-Lauve's experience, few administrators are able to identify students for whom suspension was an effective intervention.

A Parent Advocate Helps Schools to Recognize

Jenna White, a parent in Fairfax County Public Schools (FCPS), believes schools become trauma-responsive by building trauma-awareness and trauma-sensitivity throughout the community. White's focus is education at the district level with fellow PTA board members, parents, and PTA members. She explained trauma is a difficult topic; however, if the PTAs are having sessions regarding "the flu or 529 plans" there should also be sessions regarding the impact of trauma. White asks, "How many children in our schools may be abused right now? How many are hungry or homeless?" Once she presents the information, people tend to respond by sharing things going on in their communities and families.

White discussed the importance of including families and the community in the process of developing a vision for a trauma-responsive school. "Bring them in as soon as possible." She suggested starting with the school level PTA and asking the parents to come alongside and learn with the school. She encourages finding parents who will advocate for changes. "Parents know what's going on with other people's kids…We all care about our kids. So, let's all look at this together and talk about it together and go through that angle."

White stressed the importance of getting parents involved with the process of making community-wide changes within their school. "You have this wonderful focus group and force that you can unleash to support you if you can make the time for it by making it a priority."

Resources to Recognize

We selected the resources below based on research and feedback from practitioners. This list is not exhaustive, rather a starting point for educators interested in developing trauma-sensitivity in their schools to *form a strategic vision* and *communicate the vision* to stakeholders.

Title	Type	Description	QR Code/Link	Link
Every Opportunity	VIDEO	Illustrates how staff interactions with a student can impact their daily experience at school.		https://tiresources.pub/22
Implementation Assessment	REFERENCE DOCUMENT	Evidence-informed self-assessment to determine where to focus implementation efforts.		https://tiresources.pub/23
Conscious Discipline	VIDEO	A brief video about the relationship between a teacher and a student and the importance of supporting all students.		https://tiresources.pub/24
Trauma-sensitive Checklist	CHECKLIST	Two-page self-assessment to inform implementation of trauma-sensitive practices.		https://tiresources.pub/25
SAMHSA Project Aware	VIDEO	Resource designed to help schools measure progress towards becoming trauma-informed.		https://tiresources.pub/26
Care Values Alignment Tool	EVALUATION TOOL	Examination of policies, protocols, and procedures through a trauma-informed lens.		https://tiresources.pub/27
The Trauma Informed School	BOOK	Sporleder and Forbes walk readers through important considerations for becoming trauma-responsive. Practical resources and strategies are provided.		https://tiresources.pub/28
Courageous Conversations About Race	BOOK	Singleton emphasizes the importance of having uncomfortable conversations about race to discuss why achievement inequality exists.		https://tiresources.pub/29
Fostering Resilient Learners	BOOK	Souers and Hall's book walks readers through the science behind ACEs, how trauma can impact learning and behavior, and provides practical strategies for teachers. Great for a book study. Has a companion trifold.		https://tiresources.pub/30
Lost at School	BOOK	Greene reveals why many students with challenging behaviors at school continue to struggle despite traditional approaches to discipline and provide suggestions for how to reform discipline practices.		https://tiresources.pub/31

Figure 5.7 Resources to Recognize

Title	Type	Description	QR Code/Link	Link
Other People's Children	BOOK	Delpit provides multiple examples illustrating how cultural competence, implicit bias, and privilege can impact teachers' interactions with students.		https://tiresources.pub/32
Help for Billy	BOOK	Forbes illustrates how trauma can impact behavior and learning. She provides practical strategies for teachers. Excellent book for a books study. Has a companion study guide.		https://tiresources.pub/33
Framework for Understanding Poverty	BOOK	Payne provides an opportunity for readers to better understand how poverty can impact students and families. She provides practical strategies for working with students experiencing poverty.		https://tiresources.pub/34
Culturally Responsive Teaching & the Brain	BOOK	Hammond connects brain research to learning and behavior in the classroom and provides practical classroom strategies to increase culturally responsive teaching.		https://tiresources.pub/35
Reaching & Teaching Students in Poverty	BOOK	Gorski expands educators' views of how poverty can impact learning and how educators can positively impact student outcomes with specific instructional strategies.		https://tiresources.pub/36
Creating & Advocating for Trauma-Sensitive Schools	REFERENCE DOCUMENT	Follow-up document to Helping Traumatized Children Learn providing a guide for schools becoming trauma-responsive and policy recommendations.		https://tiresources.pub/37
Sources of Strength	CURRICULUM	Research-based suicide awareness and resilience program supported by peer leaders.		https://tiresources.pub/45
International Institute of Restorative Practices	WEBSITE	Comprehensive resource for restorative practices.		https://tiresources.pub/65

Figure 5.7 Continued

References

Bailey, B. (2018). The conscious discipline brain state model: A multidisciplinary approach based on three distinct brain-body states in adults and children that drive behavior. *Conscious Discipline*. Retrieved from https://consciousdiscipline.com/methodology/brain-state-model/.

Bell, H., Limberg, D., & Robinson, E. M. III (2013, April 28). Recognizing trauma in the classroom: A practical guide for educators. *Childhood Education*, *89*(3), 139–145. doi: 10.1080/00094056.2013.792629.

Collaborative for Academic, Social, and Emotional Learning. (2018). Retrieved from https://casel.org/.

Community Resilience Initiative. (2018). Our team: Teri Barila. Community Resilience Initiative. Retrieved from https://criresilient.org/about-us/our-team/.

Danzinger, S., Levav, J., & Avnaim-Pesso, L. (2011). Extraneous factors in judicial decisions. *Proceedings of the National Academy of Sciences of the United States of America,* 108. doi: 10.1073/pnas.1018033108

Forbes, H. T. (2012). *Help for billy: A beyond consequences approach to helping challenging children in the classroom.* Boulder, CO: Beyond Consequences Institute, LLC.

Ginsburg, K. (2018). The 7C's: The essential building blocks of resilience. *Fostering Resilience.* Retrieved from http://www.fosteringresilience.com/7cs/php.

Gregory, A., & Weinstein, R. S. (2008). The discipline gap and African Americans: Defiance or cooperation in the high school classroom. *Journal of School Psychology, 46*(4), 455–475. doi: 10.1016/j.jsp.2007.09.001.

Guditas, S. (2013, February 2013). Maslow's hierarchy of school needs [Web log post]. Retrieved from http://sguditus.blogspot.com/2013/02/maslows-hierarchy-of-school-needs-steve.html.

Harris, R., & Petaccio, K. (2017). From chaos to calm. *Georgia Association for Positive Support Conference.* 19. https://digitalcommons.georgiasouthern.edu/gapbs/2017/2017/19.

Kotter, J. P. (2012). *Leading change.* Boston, MA: Harvard Business School Press.

Kotter International (2019). *Kotter.* https://www.kotterinc.com/8-steps-process-for-leading-change/

Lee, H., Griffin, R. M., & Keels, M. (2018, January). *Maintaining educator well-being.* Practice Brief #4. TREP Project. Retrieved from http://docs.wixstatic.com/ugd/fc6e9a_7e863bbcdfff4e65b686f392f45c4c8d.pdf.

Losen, D., Hodson, C., Keith, M. A., Morrison, K., & Belway, S. (2015). Are we closing the discipline gap? (The Center for Civil Rights Remedies Report, February 23, 2015). Retrieved from https://www.civilrightsproject.ucla.edu/resources/projects/center-for-civil-rights-remedies/school-to-prison-folder/fede ral-reports/are-we-closing-the-school-discipline-gap/?searchterm=are%20we %20closing%20the%20discipline%20gap.

McIntosh, K. (2017). Strategies for neutralizing implicit bias in school discipline. Retrieved from http://pbisconference.org/files/2017/04/McIntosh-Implicit-Bias-2017-4-24.pdf.

McIntosh, K., & Goodman, S. (2016). *Integrated multi-tiered systems of support: Blending RTI and PBIS.* New York: Guilford Press.

Missouri Department of Mental Health and Partners. (2014). *Missouri model: A developmental framework for trauma informed approaches.* Retrieved from https://dmh.mo.gov/trauma/.

National Child Traumatic Stress Network. (2008, October). *Child toolkit for educators.* Los Angeles, CA: National Center for Child Traumatic Stress. Retrieved from https://wmich.edu/sites/default/files/attachments/u57/2013/c hild-trauma-toolkit.pdfMO%20Model%20Working%20Document%20february %202015.pdf.

National Child Traumatic Stress Network, Schools Committee. (2017). *Creating, supporting, and sustaining trauma-informed schools: A system framework.* Los Angeles, CA: National Center for Child Traumatic Stress.

National Child Traumatic Stress Network. (2018). *Who we are*. Los Angeles, CA: National Center for Child Traumatic Stress. Retrieved from https://www.nctsn.or g/about-us/who-we-are

Payne, R. K. (2018). *Emotional poverty in all demographics*. Highlands, TX: Aha! Process, Inc.

Siegel, D. J. (2010). *Mindsight: The new science of personal transformation*. New York: Bantam Books.

Substance Abuse and Mental Health Services Administration. (2014, July). SAMHSA's concept of trauma and guidance for a trauma-informed approach. Retrieved from https://store.samhsa.gov/system/files/sma14-4884.pdf.

US Department of the Navy, US Marine Corps. (2010, December). *Combat and Operational Stress Control* (NTTP 1-15M, MCRP 6-11C). Retrieved from https ://www.med.navy.mil/sites/nmcphc/Documents/health-promotion-wellness/p sychological-emotional-wellbeing/combat-operational-stress-control-nttp-115m .pdf.

White, C. C. (2017, February). Putting resilience and resilience surveys under the microscope. *Aces Too High News*. Retrieved from https://acestoohigh.com/2017 /02/05/_trashed-4/.

Wood, L. (2018, November). Putting resiliency understanding to work for youth (and you). In S. Dion (Chair), *Strengthening connections: Fostering resiliency and supporting the development of safe and healthy students from kindergarten through college*. Symposium conducted at the meeting of the Virginia Department of Criminal Justice Services, Richmond, VA.

6 Respond

Embracing Trauma-Responsive Practices

We applaud all school leaders who are creating a sense of urgency for discipline reform. You are developing a guiding coalition to **R**ealize the problem of exclusionary discipline and the impact trauma can have on students, families, and staff. You have also begun forming and communicating a strategic vision that **R**ecognizes the influence of implicit biases and trauma within your school or school division. Working with an inclusive culture that values self-reflection and courageous conversations, you must now embark on what is arguably the most challenging part of the process: determining how to **R**espond.

According to the Missouri Model, "trauma-responsive organizations have begun to change their organizational culture to highlight the role of trauma. At all levels of the organization, staff begins rethinking the routines and infrastructure of the organization" (Missouri Department of Mental Health and Partners, 2014, p. 4). The process of **R**esponding to the needs of all students involves *empowering others to act* and *generating quick wins* (Kotter, 2012).

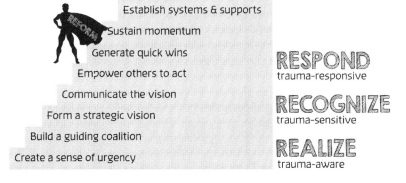

Figure 6.1 Discipline Reform Model: RESPOND (Kotter, 2012; Missouri Department of Mental Health and Partners, 2014; Substance Abuse and Mental Health Services Administration, 2014)

Role of the Principal

When a principal provides the guiding coalition and all faculty/staff with the ideas, support, and resources to be successful, the impetus for change will be contagious. Sharing promising data, frequently highlighting success stories, giving regular positive feedback, praising students, and making positive parent phone calls are some effective ways to maintain collective momentum.

Anderson, Blitz, and Saastamoinen (2015) suggest leaders must look beyond traditional "one and done" professional development. Joyce and Showers (2002) recommend classroom coaching, which increases the chance a teacher will use new practices in the classroom by 95%. Although most schools do not have staff with the sole responsibility of coaching teachers in the use of trauma-responsive practices, trauma-responsive leaders within the building can partner and support teachers daily through their own modeling, observation, and targeted feedback.

High-quality professional development for instructional assistants is also important because they often work closely with students impacted by ACEs. Finding ways to involve other support staff (e.g., bus drivers and cafeteria employees) creates an inclusive environment where all members Realize and Recognize their contribution to a trauma-responsive culture.

Purtle (2018) conducted multiple experimental studies evaluating the relationship between trauma-responsive professional development and student outcomes. The studies revealed that trauma-responsive professional development appears to improve staff knowledge, attitudes, and behaviors; however, it becomes less clear if too many initiatives can be sustained for a significant period of time. Professional development should enhance versus overwhelm teacher self-efficacy. Accordingly, some of the leaders we interviewed chose to implement one practice at a time, slowly introducing trauma-responsive practices that educate the whole child. Other leaders combined practices to best fit their school context and students' needs. All leaders used data to select practices to support their strategic vision.

Implementing Trauma-Responsive Practices

Below we provide an overview of trauma-responsive discipline practices and stories of their implementation. Each of the practices described has successfully reduced exclusionary discipline and raised student resilience. Principals and their guiding coalitions should return to Appendix D while reading this chapter and select practices that best support each vision statement, complement existing initiatives, and empower staff to become trauma-responsive. It is important to choose trauma-responsive practices that will target critical student needs and generate quick wins so teachers feel greater self-efficacy. We begin with instructional engagement.

Instructional Engagement

The most engaging teachers have the fewest discipline problems in their classrooms. They successfully develop relationships, create relevant lessons, and emphasize rigor—and always in that order.

Relationships. Forty-year educator Rita Pierson states, "Kids don't learn from people they don't like" (2013, 7:13). Indeed, teachers are the most critical factor in the process of building student resilience. The National Child Traumatic Stress Network found "school personnel are uniquely situated to identify, respond to, and be impacted by students' traumatic stress symptoms due to their central role in children's lives and their continued assessment of children's learning abilities and relationships with peers and school staff" (NCTSN, Schools Committee, 2017, p. 2). According to Downey (2008), students are more successful "when they belong to a classroom in which a teacher (a) has clear behavioral expectations, (b) conveys to students that they are personally responsible for their success, (c) creates a caring classroom community, and (d) provides opportunities for meaningful student participation" (p. 59). Pierson (2013) declares, "Every child deserves a champion, an adult who understands the power of connection, and insists they become the best that they can possibly be" (7:14).

Relevance. Culturally relevant instruction promotes student interest and positive ethnic-racial identities that reduce achievement gaps. According to Byrd (2016), culturally relevant teaching should combine high expectations, cultural competence, and critical consciousness. High expectations show a belief in students' ability to take responsibility for their own success, while scaffolding instruction to support it. Cultural competence shows respect for and inclusivity of students' communities and customs to bridge experiences, ideas, and familiar content with new learning. Critical consciousness encourages students to identify local problems and to engage in active problem solving. When high expectations, cultural competence, and critical consciousness are combined, students are empowered with life skills, dignity, and the ability to handle more academic rigor.

Rigor. According to McIntosh (2017), "Students with low academic skills are more likely to exhibit unwanted behavior in schools, and vice versa" (Author Comments in presentation at the National PBIS Conference). Conversely, students who are demonstrating academic success are more likely to have productive behavior, and vice versa. When teachers differentiate instruction to a student's ability level, they are able to scaffold instruction in a positive direction. Student success leads to greater confidence and the ability to meet increasingly higher expectations. Student engagement thus enables more rigorous instruction. Rigor means much more than passing standardized state exams. After 30 years of teaching to the test, schools are now turning to deeper learning, rigor that is both relational and relevant. For example, the Virginia Department of Education (VDOE), is encouraging teachers to develop the five Cs: communication, collaboration, critical thinking, creativity, and citizenship (VDOE, 2020). By approaching rigor through a broader lens, teachers can engage students more personally and develop life readiness skills. Student discipline is a life readiness skill.

Modeling and Teaching Discipline

While planning and delivering engaging instruction, teachers should also model and teach discipline. According to Bailey (2018a), "the biggest threat to a child's sense of safety is an out-of-control adult" (para. 1). Yelling, belittling, shaming, publicly humiliating students, or "any classroom management or discipline system that fails to address the conscious awareness and emotional intelligence of the adult is ultimately doomed" (Bailey, 2018a, para. 4). When disciplining children, teachers must not lose their patience or be visibly reactive; instead, they should self-regulate their own behavior and consciously model desired behaviors for their students (Bailey, 2018a).

The Seven Powers for Conscious Adults (Figure 6.2) advises how teachers can model resilience for students. According to Bailey (2018a), the seven powers help teachers become more conscious of their reactions to conflict and "to stay in control of themselves and in charge of children in a manner that models the same skills we seek to teach" (para. 8). These powers enable teachers to **R**espond "in a way that helps children move from the resistant, lower centers of their brain to the more cooperative, higher centers" (Bailey, 2018b, para. 5).

Bailey has also identified seven *Conscious Discipline Skills* (Figure 6.3) to teach children "the social-emotional and communication skills necessary to manage themselves, resolve conflict, prevent bullying, and develop prosocial behaviors" (para. 3). Teachers can provide direct instruction to students in prosocial behaviors and reinforce with practice, encouragement, and correction as needed. As with academics, when behavior problems are complex or chronic, specialized interventions may be necessary. Logical and consistent consequences are also important to ensure student accountability. However, consequences must be given in a context of teaching and learning, not shaming. The goal is to help students take responsibility for their actions and give them the opportunity to redeem themselves.

Power	Big Idea	Goal
Perception	No one can make you angry without your permission.	To take responsibility for our own upset.
Unity	We are all in this together.	To perceive compassionately, and offer compassion to others and to ourselves.
Attention	Whatever we focus on, we get more of.	To create images of expected behavior in a child's brain.
Free Will	The only person you can change is you.	Learning to connect and guide instead of force and coerce.
Acceptance	The moment is as it is.	To learn to respond to what life offers instead of attempting to make the world go our way.
Love	Choose to see the best in others.	Seeing the best in others keep us in the higher centers of our brain so we can consciously respond instead of unconsciously react to life events.
Intention	Mistakes are opportunities to learn.	To teach a new skill rather than punishing others for lacking skills we think they should possess by now.

Figure 6.2 The Seven Powers for Conscious Adults (Bailey, 2018a)

Conscious Discipline Skills	Life/Communication Skills	Values
Composure	Anger management, delay of gratification	Integrity
Encouragement	Pro-social skills: kindness, caring, helpfulness	Interdependence, optimism, gratitude
Assertiveness	Bully prevention, healthy boundaries	Respect for self and others
Choices	Impulse control, goal achievement	Persistence
Empathy	Emotional regulation, perspective-taking	Honoring diversity, honesty
Positive Intent	Cooperation, problem-solving	Compassion, generosity
Consequences	Learning from your mistakes	Responsibility

Figure 6.3 Conscious Discipline Skills (Bailey, 2018b)

Figure 6.4 visually represents four types of student discipline. The x-axis measures *Support*, the y-axis measures *Expectations*. Low Support, Low Expectations (Neglectful) provides students with little discipline to the extent that it is detrimental to the student. Low Support, High Expectations (Punitive) emphasizes rule-following for the sake of rules and the punishments for breaking them. High Support, Low Expectations (Permissive) provides students with little accountability or personal responsibility. High Support, High Expectations (Restorative) provides students with accountability while developing resilience and responsibility. Trauma-responsive practices should be implemented within a Restorative framework of discipline.

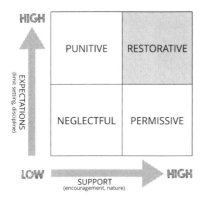

Figure 6.4 The Social Discipline Window (Wachtel, 2009)

Routines, Procedures, and Student Choice

Another powerful strategy for supporting *all* students is to provide structured and predictable daily routines, procedures, and transitions. For instance, the faculty and staff at Ecoff Elementary, Chesterfield County Public Schools, schedule a morning meeting circle time for 20-minutes at the beginning of each school day, and then again for five minutes in the afternoon. Students have an opportunity to express and share their feelings with one another and can choose what and how they communicate, participate, and learn.

At Clark Elementary, Charlottesville City Public Schools, early childhood teachers use pictorial illustrated visuals to communicate daily schedules. *Dana Carrico*, teacher of three-year-olds, noted, "I didn't change the schedule for the first six weeks. It was exactly the same because [the students] need to really get it embedded in their head, and become comfortable with that so they know it is safe. This is what [our day is] going to be, this is what our schedule is going to be." Once students are comfortable with the schedule, teachers can revise the schedule and introduce a new picture. "I think it is really beneficial for all kids with trauma so they know what's coming next, because if you're coming from an unpredictable environment, that's very comforting."

Cultural Competence Training

Cultural competence is "having an awareness of one's own cultural identity and views about difference, and the ability to learn and build on the varying cultural and community norms of students and their families" (National

Education Association, 2018, para. 3). For educators, cultural competence training is needed to recognize implicit bias. Many professionals do not realize some of their statements or actions may inadvertently and negatively impact a student.

Edwards (2016) found that Black students are much more likely to be suspended or expelled in homogeneously White schools or Black schools. They concluded that diverse schools with greater racial familiarity may heighten cultural competence and decrease exclusionary discipline. As discussed in Chapter 1, Black schools have statistically higher rates of free and reduced lunch, and ACEs are often associated with poverty. Cultural competence of poverty should be a priority in these schools because it avoids deficit-thinking and promotes student resilience through a trauma-responsive lens. According to Payne and Welch (2015), "If these schools transitioned to social engagement over social control, they would be more likely to reduce exclusionary discipline, reintegrate 'problem' students, create a sense of community that enhances students' bonds to school, and decrease student involvement in 'delinquent activities'" (p. 558). Most importantly, these schools would build student resilience.

Jessica Hawthorne, director of programs at Virginia Center for Inclusive Communities (VCIC) described "cultural proficiency training" as a process of changing culture over time and should include regular positive feedback. Its ultimate goal is to promote and celebrate *equity literacy*. She referenced Gorski's *Equity Literacy Framework* (2014) which identifies five abilities and associated knowledge/skills educators need to be able to avoid educational disparities and advocate for educational equity. Hawthorne noted the framework's flexibility and usefulness. We note the framework's striking similarity to the four **R**s (see Figure 6.5).

---

1. The ability to **recognize** even the subtlest biases and inequities,

2. The ability to **respond** skillfully and equitably to biases and inequities in immediate term,

3. The ability to **redress** biases and inequities by understanding and addressing them at their institutional roots,

4. The ability to **actively cultivate** equity by applying an equity commitment to every decision, and

5. The ability to **sustain** equity efforts even in the face of discomfort or resistance.

Figure 6.5 Five Abilities of Equity Literacy (Gorski, 2014)

De-Escalation Techniques

De-escalation techniques are specifically meant to help students re-regulate their emotions. In terms of discipline, *Heather Forbes*, licensed clinical social worker, emphasizes "responding instead of reacting" (Forbes, 2012, p. 79). Teachers and administrators should not view students as "good" or "bad" but as "regulated" or "dysregulated" (Forbes, 2012, p. 9). A regulated child is in homeostasis, a balanced or resilient state, whereas a dysregulated child is distressed and behaves in a state of either hyper-arousal or hypo-arousal (Forbes, 2012). When teachers and administrators need to quickly respond when students do "flip their lids," Payne (2018) recommends several helpful strategies.

1. Recognize that the meltdown is the result of an unregulated, unintegrated brain response, not personal disrespect.
2. Contain the behavior so no one is hurt.
3. Use effective calming techniques to soothe the child. Have the student get a drink of water to metabolize the cortisol their body has produced. Encourage the student to tell a future story ("What do you want to do?" "What do you want to be?"). Use tapping and touch (e.g., holding the student's hand), and asking the student to look up. Generally, when humans look up, the brain is processing visual information. When their eyes move between the ears the brain is processing auditory information. When they look down the brain is processing emotional or kinesthetic information. Asking a student to look up helps to calm and transition an emotional response.
4. Use a breathing technique (e.g., slow breath in, hold and count to five, slow breath out, repeat).
5. Put left hand over heart, right hand over stomach and rub at the same time to release serotonin.
6. Directly teach Daniel Siegel's hand model to students (See Figure 6.6). When students understand what is happening in their brains when they lose control, they can better participate in the process of self-regulation ("Let's get back to your upstairs brain"). (Payne, 2018, p. 17)

For students who are dysregulated, behavioral issues in the classroom may be manifestations of trauma. Students who cannot internally regulate require external regulations beyond consequences (Forbes, 2012). Discipline must include proactive measures including:

1. a safe, nurturing, compassionate, and attuned relationship with a regulated adult;
2. an inclusive sense of belonging; non-threatening body language (e.g., squatting, sitting);

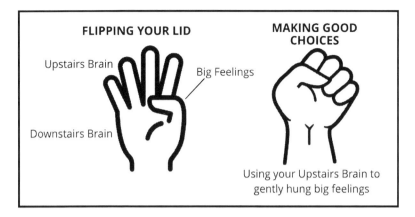

Figure 6.6 Dan Siegel's Hand Model (Siegel, 2012)

3. avoiding fear-based motivation (e.g., "If you don't do your work then ___ will happen");
4. avoiding sticker charts that may cause anxiety (e.g., losing stickers);
5. giving students the opportunity to voice their feelings without judgment or correction;
6. giving emotional space (calming room, a walk with an adult);
7. giving frequent opportunity for movement and brain breaks;
8. involving parent support versus parent fear;
9. providing homework options when home is a stressful environment;
10. assessing student processes versus student outcomes. (Forbes, 2012)

It is essential to emphasize that physical restraint of students is *not* a de-escalation technique. Physical restraint can lead to re-traumatization and, in some cases, death. Many school divisions require that school administrators and teacher leaders be formally trained in workplace de-escalation techniques such as the Mandt System for crisis prevention and emergency physical intervention training (see Resources at the end of the chapter).

Family and Community Engagement

Families play a vital role in creating a plan and selecting interventions to best support their child. They may help identify challenges, triggers, and potential solutions. Collaborating with families helps staff gain better insight into a student's background and history. Mayworm and Sharkey (2014) suggest including school psychologists to help understand, identify, and support a student who has experienced ACEs.

School administrators can also encourage communication and collaborative problem solving with families. Many teachers feel apprehensive about communicating with families. Some schools require teachers to document a certain number of positive phone calls home each week. They keep a record of which students receive the calls to ensure every student receives at least one positive contact every few weeks. Other schools who traditionally do not have a large number of parents attend conferences set up home visits with families instead.

School administrators should provide training and opportunities for teachers to practice handling difficult parent conversations, and should make phone calls or attend conferences with teachers. Figure 6.7 provides guidance on "do"s and "don't"s of parent communication.

Olivya Wilson, resiliency project parent engagement coordinator, Richmond Public Schools (RPS) and GR-SCAN, referenced the Flamboyan Foundation as a resource she has used to support teachers and parents to facilitate effective communication while building positive relationships with families. The slogan on the Flamboyan Foundation website reads, "When authentic relationships between families and educators are built, everyone wins." The foundation provides a wealth of resources designed to open the lines of communication between parents and teachers. Home visits are driven by appreciative inquiry where school faculty approach conversations with families with a strengths-based mindset. "Instead of asking what is wrong, use the power of inquiry to ask what is right?" (Meyers, 2018,

DO NOT:	DO:
Blame the Child - "I have told John that he needs to stop hitting but he chooses to keep putting his hands on other kids."	Consider Your Role - "I am working on ways to help John learn to use nice hands. I want to discuss the strategies I've been using and get your feedback."
Assume Status - "Your child's behavior is not appropriate for 3rd grade and he knows that. Please teach him these behavior expectations at home."	Assume the Parent is your Partner - "I know that we both want John to be successful so there a few behaviors that we need to work on to help him be his best."
Give Attribute Praise - "Your child is smart."	Give Specific Examples - "Your child takes initiative with problem solving. For example..."
Shame the Child - "John hit someone today and he isn't even sorry about it. He will miss recess for today and he'll be in ISS if this happens again."	Work on a Plan with the Child and Parent - "John and I have just finished having a discussion about hitting other students. Here's what we decided would have been a better choice and how he can fix what he has done. What would you like to add Mom?"
Use Educational Jargon - "Your child is in Tier 2 for RtI based on SAM data."	Provide a Clear Explanation - "Recent math assessment results show that John will benefit from a math intervention group."

Figure 6.7 Parent Communication Hacks (Minch, 2019)

slide 6). Below are a few practical strategies for school leaders who decide to encourage faculty to go on home visits.

- Ask teachers to go in pairs.
- Set initial expectations for visits to several students.
- Use established parent-teacher conference times or pre-service days.
- Find ways to compensate teachers for home visits.
- Have a "hub" staffed by a school social worker.
- Prepare teachers and answer questions.
- Print maps/directions.
- Print notes to leave on the door if no one is home.
- Schedule a time to debrief the experience with teachers. (Meyers, 2018, slide 16)

Although home visits can be an effective strategy to increase family engagement, participation in visits should be voluntary, or equitably built into teacher work requirements and compensation.

Multi-Tiered Systems of Supports (MTSS)

Multi-Tiered Systems of Supports (MTSS) seek to proactively respond to varying degrees of student needs with integrated strategies to serve the whole child (Fairbanks, Sugai, Guardino, & Lathrop, 2007). Most commonly, tiered academic systems are called Response to Intervention (RTI), while tiered behavior systems are called Positive Behavioral Interventions and Supports (PBIS) (McIntosh & Goodman, 2016). Many states and school divisions across the nation are working to integrate mental health services into MTSS. Tier 1 strategies are implemented schoolwide, while Tier 2 and 3 interventions are designed for students who need increasing levels of support as indicated by data. Within an effective MTSS, 100% of students receive Tier 1 universal supports. Approximately five to 15% of students require Tier 2 interventions to provide them with explicit instruction on select academic, behavioral, or social-emotional skills (e.g., making inferences from a passage, asking for help, dealing with anger appropriately) (Peterson et al., 2004). Tier 2 interventions are provided to small groups of students, typically no more than 15 at one time (NCTSN, Schools Committee, 2017; Peterson et al., 2004). Tier 3 interventions are for approximately one to seven% of a student population who have been identified as having serious or chronic behavior, academic, or mental health needs (Peterson et al., 2004). Consistent implementation of Tier 1 supports are the foundation for an effective MTSS.

School leaders can determine the effectiveness of their Tier 1 academic, behavioral, and social-emotional supports by reviewing grade level or schoolwide data. For example, if more than 20% of eighth graders in a school fail the end-of-course English assessment, it is likely there is an issue with the whole group (Tier 1) instructional delivery. If more than 20% of students in an elementary school are receiving one or more office discipline referral (ODR) each year, it is likely there is an issue with initial instruction and reinforcement of school-wide behavior expectations. Ineffective Tier 1 practices can lead to the over identification of students requiring tiered interventions which demand more staff and time than many schools can support.

When implementing an MTSS, it is important to avoid identifying students by Tier. It is common to hear teachers and administrators refer to students as Tier 1, Tier 2, or Tier 3 kids. Labeling students this way can promote and perpetuate fixed mindsets about students' abilities. Educators tier supports, not students. The purpose of an MTSS is to provide students with opportunities to gain the skills they need to be successful so they no longer require intervention. Students who receive tiered interventions continue to receive access to Tier 1 practices. School leaders need to establish decision-making rules to inform movement of students to and from each tier.

Although teachers in trauma-responsive schools **R**ealize the impact of trauma on learning and **R**ecognize signs of trauma, it is important to distinguish the role of teachers and mental health professionals. Most educators are not licensed therapists but need to be able to identify when a student needs support and how to connect him or her to appropriate service providers (Morrow, 1987). Trauma-informed staff such as school counselors, psychologists, or social workers can help identify students who require Tier 3 mental health supports and collaborate with community partners to find appropriate interventions. Many schools use some form of a Student Support Team (SST) to make data-driven decisions about student interventions (Steinberg & Lacoe; 2017). Schools need to have personnel who

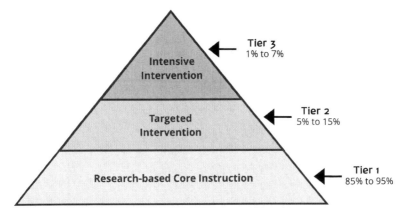

Figure 6.8 Multi-Tiered Systems of Supports (McIntosh & Goodman, 2016)

are prepared to manage any critical events or situations that could arise (NCTSN, Schools Committee, 2017).

In Virginia, schools use the Virginia Threat Assessment as a Tier 3 intervention to identify and support students who demonstrate a potential harm to self or others. Welsh and Little (2018) highlighted a study which evaluated the impact of the Virginia Threat Assessment on out-of-school suspensions (OSS). The study revealed a "53% decrease in long-term suspensions and a 79% reduction in bullying infractions" (Welsh & Little, 2018, p. 779). A more extensive study involving nearly 2,000 students revealed that students who were evaluated through the Virginia Threat Assessment were less likely to be suspended from school (Welsh & Little, 2018). This research suggests schools which take a proactive therapeutic approach to supporting students will see a reduction in exclusionary discipline.

As school leaders begin to select trauma-responsive practices to implement in their schools, the development of MTSS can provide structure to organize change efforts.

Positive Behavioral Interventions and Supports (PBIS)

Positive Behavioral Interventions and Supports (PBIS) is a research-based MTSS to organize behavior and sometimes social-emotional supports for students. Tier 1 behavior supports include effective communication, social competence, and self-management skills (Steinberg & Lacoe, 2017). Bradshaw, Mitchell, O'Brennan, and Leaf (2010) measured the influence PBIS has on school culture, discipline, and student outcomes. The study revealed that schools where educators were trained in PBIS demonstrated a significant reduction in the percentage of students who received an ODR. When schools implementing PBIS were compared to the national average, PBIS schools demonstrated fewer major ODRs per 100 students (Bradshaw et al., 2010). In alignment with the Every Student Succeeds Act (ESSA) requirements, schools implementing PBIS use research-based strategies to prevent student behaviors from interfering with learning (PBIS, 2018; US Department of Education, 2018). A key Tier 1 strategy is to clearly identify and communicate expectations across all settings (e.g., classrooms, bus, cafeteria, playground, gym). School leaders should aim to have at least 80% of the students accurately identify the behavioral expectations. This goal is accomplished by positively labeling, posting, and explicitly teaching the desired behaviors while also modeling and reinforcing the expectations (PBIS, 2018).

Some faculty or staff may criticize PBIS because it lacks consequences for negative student behavior. Others may argue that PBIS only focuses on external incentives to motivate students, or may incorrectly use clip charts to shame students when they misbehave in front of their peers (Lewis,

2013). These common fallacies emphasize the importance of a strategic roll-out of PBIS. School staff must have time and opportunities to switch from traditional consequence-driven discipline and learn new discipline procedures which teach students replacement behaviors. Teachers need to practice providing positive, timely, specific feedback to students rather than focusing on tangible rewards to drive behavior change. Professional development should give strategies to build meaningful relationships with students, establish clear expectations, teach routines, procedures, and expected behaviors as often as needed throughout the year (Algozzine et al., 2014; Lewis, 2013; PBIS, 2018; Safe and Responsive Schools, 2018).

Many school leaders implementing PBIS establish a school-based PBIS Team and use the Tiered Fidelity Inventory (TFI) to guide the process. The TFI is divided into evaluation features for all three tiers and provides a brief overview of the essential structures of PBIS. The link to the TFI is at the end of this chapter.

In 2005, 50% of students at Cedar Lee Middle School, Fauquier County Public Schools (FCPS) had received at least one ODR. The principal, *Steve Parker*, **R**ealized and **R**ecognized that discipline practices needed to change. Parker invested in the implementation of Tier 1 PBIS and began problem solving ways to better support students being punished for minor offenses. During a five-year period, the implementation of Tier 1 PBIS decreased the number of students receiving at least one ODR to 36%, a 14% reduction.

Providing students with a faculty supported conflict resolution program is an example of a Tier 2 PBIS intervention (NCTSN, Schools Committee, 2017). Students, even at the high school level, have difficulty resolving conflicts with little to no support. Therefore, students can receive targeted support to learn how to resolve potential or existing conflicts. Erinn J. Green, co-author and assistant principal, Prince Edward County Public Schools, has used peer mediation throughout her career to help students resolve conflict. "This is a common strategy used when students are affected by interactions on social media. The students involved are spoken to separately and then brought together for an honest conversation facilitated by a trusted adult. Providing a safe space for students to develop empathy lasts long beyond the initial conversation."

Check-in, Check-out (CICO) is another example of a Tier 2 behavior intervention in which students check-in with a trusted adult at least twice a day to set, assess, and remind students of their daily goals. Together, the students' teachers collect data using a brief assessment tool throughout the day to evaluate the students' progress meeting goals. The assessment tool often includes student self-reflections as well. Check-In, Check-Out is an effective way to encourage, reward, and hold students accountable for daily successes on individual Behavior Intervention Plans. Checking-in at the beginning of the day sets the stage for starting a new day with a clean slate. Checking-out gives a student the opportunity to take pride in their good behavior or to debrief and discuss why their day was not successful. The data collected can be used to communicate with families, coordinate with educators, and make recommendations for further interventions if needed. *Kirk Eggleston*, co-author and principal of Gayton Elementary, Henrico County Public Schools (HCPS), has seen CICO work wonders with students who are often referred to the office for classroom disruptions. "CICO gives kids an ally and proponent who rewards them and holds them accountable. Many students are crying out for such a person. The CICO relationship makes an otherwise disconnected student feel valued and eager to please."

Stephanie Poe, co-author and principal of Hopewell High School, Hopewell City Public Schools, initiated a Tier 2 and 3 PBIS strategy for marijuana possession/use. Typically, students were suspended 10 days upon the first incident, and suspended for another 10 days on any subsequent incidents with a referral to the Central Discipline Committee. The Committee could decide to place the students in an alternative school or to a contracted outplacement school. The Committee could also choose to require a hearing before the School Board for possible expulsion. Poe was concerned that suspending these students effectively sent them home to smoke more marijuana. Instead of a 10-day suspension, she provided parents and students with the option of attending drug counseling with a counselor from the local Community Service Board, and subsequently with a full-time in-house mental health counselor. The total time remains at 10 days, so the student might have one day of suspension and nine days of counseling, or two days suspension and eight days of counseling. The student and counselor work together to determine when those sessions will take place. The counseling sessions are confidential, information is not shared with parents or the administrators, unless the information falls under topics that counselors must report such as child abuse. According to Poe, every student who has been caught under the influence of or in possession of drugs has chosen this option, as did their parents. After participating in the counseling, Hopewell High students have had no recidivism. The school is continuing to use this process and is expanding the reasons to choose counseling over punishment with the in-house mental health counselor.

Social-Emotional Learning (SEL)

Many schools embed SEL in Tier 1 core instruction. Ashdown and Bernard (2012) discovered that only 40% of the children entering school have the social-emotional skills necessary to be successful in kindergarten. Students who lack social-emotional skills display lower levels of competence in their confidence, persistence, and organization, as well as general academic achievement (Ashdown & Bernard, 2012). Social-emotional learning strategies focus on supporting and developing positive teacher-student relationships, as well as building strong student-student relationships (Yang et al., 2018). Yang et al. (2018) discovered a positive correlation between supportive peer relationships and student engagement at school.

In 1994, the Collaborative for Academic, Social, and Emotional Learning (CASEL) was founded to support the integration of SEL into public schools from early childhood through high school (CASEL, 2018). Social-emotional learning teaches students how to "recognize and understand their emotions, feel empathy, make decisions, and build and maintain relationships" (CASEL, 2018, para. 1). In 2017, Taylor, Oberle, Durlak, and Weissberg completed a meta-analysis of 82 different SEL interventions. Students who received SEL instruction demonstrated greater social and emotional competencies and prosocial behaviors and attitudes six months to 18 years after participating. Additionally, the meta-analysis revealed a 6% increase in high school graduation rates, an 11% increase in college graduation rates, and a decrease in mental health disorders, drug use, pregnancy, and involvement in the juvenile justice system (Taylor et al., 2017). Although the evidence is compelling, many educators have not made time for structured SEL in the instructional day. Some educators blame the pressure of standardized assessments and the ever expanding curriculum demands handed down from state departments of education. However, trauma-responsive educators acknowledge the investment in SEL every day increases instructional time because there are fewer interruptions due to disruptive behavior (Nixon & Keels, 2018; Taylor et al., 2017).

Social-emotional learning practices span all three tiers and grade levels. Morning meetings are a common Tier 1 SEL practice in which teachers spend the first 15–20 minutes of every day to welcome students, share experiences, facilitate activities to foster a sense of community, and integrate a morning message (Rosen, 2018). Secondary school leaders may implement SEL instruction at varied times of the day or week depending on school-specific needs. Some division and school leaders invest in packaged SEL curriculum, but there are some free SEL curricula available such as Sanford Harmony (see Resources).

Joshua Cole was very careful when introducing Ecoff Elementary, Chesterfield County Public Schools, to the SEL curriculum, Caring School Community (CSC). Many teachers were still struggling with the implementation of PBIS; therefore, Cole recognized adding another program could be overwhelming. He creatively introduced SEL to his school by combining it with PBIS, calling it P. BISSEL. He referenced a famous rapper who combined his real name and nickname to become P. Diddy. This strategy helped with teacher buy-in. Cole selected six pilot teachers from 14 volunteers, empowering them to lead the way. The six attended training sessions on how to use the resources in the CSC curriculum. Following the successful implementation of the pilot program, Cole expanded training to the rest of the staff, including instructional assistants, cafeteria workers, and bus drivers.

Bridget Manuel, third grade teacher, described her class's morning meetings as "a very positive, an open dialogue moment." Her students are developing a personal growth mindset, improving academically, and resolving peer conflicts. "The students feel good on the inside, they glow, and you can see it in everything that they do."

Mindfulness

Professional development on mindfulness is often integrated with SEL curricula as students and educators improve self-awareness. Mindfulness includes explicit instruction of strategies (e.g., breathing) to improve stress management and self-control, develop healthy relationships, and make positive choices about eating, sleep, and exercise to improve overall health and well-being (Davidson, 2018). Mindfulness can be taught at all three tiers or as a targeted intervention.

Many schools have created "sensory" rooms to provide space and strategies for students who are dysregulated to de-escalate through mindfulness. These rooms can also be used by faculty and staff. When training teachers in schools, *Denise Powers*, lead early childhood specialist, Circle Preschool Program, will ask if there is a space to go to feel safe and regulated. "Kids can be triggered by [being] crowded or overly stimulated," and they require a place to diffuse. She said it is important to determine who can be there to help the child co-regulate. If the teacher is alone in the room, Powers suggested having a plan for ensuring someone is always available to help the student co-regulate.

Ram Bhagat, manager of school climate and culture strategy, explained that Richmond Public Schools (RPS) have developed "optimal healing spaces," or mindfulness rooms, based on work by Holistic Life in Baltimore, Maryland. These mindfulness rooms include things such as yoga mats, jump back chairs, lava lamps to help students self-regulate and de-stress, and staffing. Teachers can complete a referral to have a mindfulness-trained staff member lead a lesson for their class. Bhagat explained that Holistic Life originally implemented mindfulness rooms in Baltimore Public Schools (BPS) to help with stress, trauma, and dysregulation, which he calls "social arrhythmia," and "communities out of balance" where disconnection, mistrust, and alienation are common. Through the use of mindfulness rooms in BPS, suspensions in one elementary school were eliminated. According to Bhagat, BPS also "discovered students began reciprocal teaching, keeping each other in check." In other words, mindfulness rooms taught students how to help themselves and one another.

Ashley Williams, owner of Bare Soul Yoga, discussed the importance of family engagement in mindfulness training. Parents of children who participate in her lessons report how effective mindfulness practices are in teaching their children to handle difficult situations. Communication with parents and families regarding ACEs and trauma-responsive practices, such as mindfulness, helps families understand the purpose and encourages them to use what is being taught at home.

Restorative Practices and Restorative Justice

Human nature drives individuals who have been harmed by another person to seek retribution; however, punishment often leaves victims and perpetrators with unresolved feelings (Sullivan & Tifft, 2001). Restorative justice shifts the focus from punishment to reconciliation and a sense of belonging. "Restorative practices are based on restorative justice principles rather than punishment" and provide structured opportunities for both parties to provide restitution, find a resolution, and reconcile the relationship (Center for Restorative Process, 2018, para. 3). In a school environment, restitution can include the replacement of an item that was stolen or broken, but often involves some type of community service to give back to the school. Learning how to support students and teachers through this process requires professional development.

Restorative practices challenge traditional school discipline because the focus is relationship-based rather than rule-based (Payne & Welch, 2015). The focus on relationships does not mean eliminating consequences. On the contrary, the emphasis is on developing empathy for those impacted while maintaining consistent behavioral expectations (PBIS, 2018). Common restorative practices include restorative chats, restorative circles, student conferences, peer mediation, and family or group decision-making conferences. Successful implementation of restorative practices across tiers reduces recidivism and increases academic achievement (Center for Restorative Process, 2018). Restorative practices require a whole school approach where community members, parents, educators, and students believe discipline is an opportunity to teach self-reflection, empathy, and self-awareness to improve relationships, develop a sense of community, and build resilience (Romero, Robertson, & Warner, 2018). Restorative practices are a mindset. Appendix E provides a *Restorative Justice Mindset*

Survey to help lead all stakeholders toward a restorative and collective approach to student discipline.

Bob Garrity, owner of Garrity Mediation & Consulting, is an expert in training educators to implement restorative practices and restorative justice. He described the difference between restorative practices and restorative justice.

> Restorative practices should focus on the proactive piece, the community building piece, the classroom circles, the teacher language, the teacher-student relationships, the student-student group relationships. [Restorative justice] is high on accountability, [and not] soft on crime. It requires a commitment to change the behavior which caused the harm and requires a means of restoring the relationship with the person harmed and/or the community.

According to Garrity, instituting restorative practice and restorative justice in schools significantly reduces suspensions. Both seek to help students learn responsibility and empathy within the school community by "building community in the classroom" and teaching expected behaviors through inclusionary practices, rather than simply punishing students through exclusionary practices. Garrity shared numerous examples of schools and teachers who have instituted restorative practice and/or restorative justice within the school or classrooms. He stated the schools and teachers have not only seen reductions in discipline issues and bullying, but they have also seen significant increases on state test scores. "If kids feel heard, kids feel respected, kids feel trusted, and they can feel like they're in a trusting environment, they're going to be more apt to participate."

Restorative In-School Suspension (ISS)

A common Tier-2 discipline intervention is in-school suspension (ISS). Unfortunately, most ISS models "can be little more than window-dressing designed to pull down out-of-school suspension (OSS) numbers" (In-school suspension: A learning tool, 2018, para. 3). Some school divisions have simply replaced OSS with ISS, exchanging an off-site form of exclusion with an on-site one (Gonzalez, 2012).

Recommendations for trauma-responsive ISS stem from sound research that either precedes or dissents from discipline practices during the zero-tolerance era. Morris and Howard (2003), citing Short's (1988) research, identified three types of ISS programs: punitive, academic, and therapeutic. The punitive model "is based on the belief that students misbehave because they want to cause trouble within the classroom and that punishment will eliminate misbehavior" (Morris & Howard, 2003, p. 156). Students are detained with minimal communication or assistance for an average of three to five days (Morris & Howard, 2003). The academic model "assumes that discipline problems arise when students have learning difficulties that cause them frustration and that their behavior will improve with instruction in basic skills, ultimately resulting in academic growth" (Morris & Howard, 2003, p. 156). The academic model provides diagnostic assessment, individual learning goals, and remedial instruction by a skilled teacher (Morris & Howard, 2003). A third model, the therapeutic model, is "designed to help students develop problem-solving skills that should lead to appropriate behavior changes" (Morris & Howard, 2003, p. 156).

Morris and Howard (2003) suggested the most effective design for an ISS program should be differentiated for each student with elements of the academic and therapeutic models. They described a working example at a middle school where a certified teacher built relationships with individual students to assess and address academic and therapeutic needs. During a typical day, the ISS teacher:

- helped each student to physically organize his or her notebooks and locker;
- assisted each student with a time management plan for completing homework and unfinished work;
- ensured each student completed assigned academic work for full credit;
- taught social skills lessons;
- taught character skills lessons;
- helped each student to take ownership of his or her actions;
- helped each student to identify and own the problem;
- helped each child to brainstorm alternative ways of dealing with a similar problem in the future;
- brought in the counselor for group or individual discussion;
- scheduled follow-up conferences with each student after five days of return to the regular classroom to check on student progress. (Morris & Howard, 2003, p. 156)

The ISS teacher should be trained with restorative practices to help students improve self-image, communicate, problem-solve, and understand what behaviors are acceptable and unacceptable in a school environment. The model also includes staff development for teachers, parenting skills, home and school survival training for students, referral to outside mental health services, and monitoring of student behavior, both positive and negative, after leaving the ISS program (Morris & Howard, 2003).

This model is consistent with Gootman's (1998) recommendation that ISS teachers should not serve as a "sergeant at arms" but as a supportive resource of "immediate and long-term intervention" (p. 39). Stewart Kline (2016) suggested, "Restorative practices present schools with an opportunity to respectfully respond to students' inappropriate behavior, while offering an inclusive, educational, non-punitive approach to make things right for everyone involved" (p. 100).

Establish only Administrators can make ISS Referrals. To make things right, schools must redefine the protocols of ISS to seek inclusion versus exclusion (Sullivan, 1989). The most important protocol to change is that only administrators should determine if the student's conduct warrants ISS to avoid inconsistency and subjectivity by various teachers (Vavrus & Cole, 2002). A teacher's office referral is a request for a Tier 2 discipline intervention; at that level, the administrator may assign or not assign ISS in the context of student (versus teacher) need and adherence to division guidelines. Reserving ISS as a Tier 2 response will "avoid the use of ISS as a first response to minor behavior problems that might abdicate teacher responsibility for discipline in the classroom" (Sullivan, 1989, p. 35). If teachers are allowed to refer students to ISS, they should first document several prior interventions with an administrator.

Develop and Communicate an ISS Mission Statement. Sheets (1996) recommended a second protocol change. The principal should develop an ISS mission statement together with the full faculty. The process of developing a mission statement creates buy-in to the inclusionary redefinition of ISS philosophy while it clearly outlines the age appropriateness, structure, policies, record-keeping, and procedures of ISS referrals (Sheets, 1996; Sullivan, 1989). A copy of the collective ISS mission should be distributed to each member of the faculty and administration (Sullivan, 1989). This mission statement can be embedded into your strategic vision, with the clear distinction that ISS is a restorative versus punitive intervention.

Ensure ISS Meets the Needs of SWD. A third protocol must be to protect SWD. Students with disabilities are overrepresented in ISS for a variety of reasons. Some SWD have difficulty responding to social cues, making well-informed decisions, and navigating complex social interactions (Zhang, Katsiyannis, & Herbst, 2004). If special education students are continually returning to ISS, the IEP team should determine if the behavior is a manifestation of the disability, complete a Functional Behavior Assessment (FBA) and create a Behavior Intervention Plan (BIP). Relevant data should help determine if the student is receiving instruction in their least restrictive environment (Ryan, Katsiyannis, Peterson, & Chmelar, 2007).

Limit the Student-Teacher Ratio and Have Defined Goals. A fourth protocol should limit the size and scope of ISS. When designing a restorative ISS program, "decide the maximum number of students that the ISS facility can suitably accommodate and that the in-school suspension teacher can effectively supervise" (Sullivan, 1989, p. 38); preferably, no more than 8–12 students at one time (Vanderslice, 1999). Each student should have relevant academic instruction with remedial support for full academic credit, a portion of the day devoted to restorative practices such as counseling and problem solving, and a supportive re-entry plan that includes follow up communication with administration, classroom teachers, counselors, parents, and the student (Gootman, 1998; Morris & Howard, 2003; Sullivan 1989). Work completion and student responsibility should be emphasized for every student in ISS (Sullivan, 1989); however, accomplishing either objective requires the ISS program to be individualized to each student (Sheets, 1996). Restitution and conflict mediation should be used during ISS for students who have had physical altercations with one another (Delisio, 2007).

Hire, Train, and Compensate ISS Specialists. A fifth protocol requirement deals with staffing. To meet the academic and restorative needs of students needing inclusionary intervention, an ISS program requires hiring and funding of a full-time certified teacher who, ideally, has had experience in counseling or teaching special education (Dickinson & Miller, 2006; Sheets, 1996). Delisio (2007) recommended ISS teachers should be trained in mediation and conflict resolution.

Create an ISS Team. To support the ISS teacher, school counselors, social workers, and psychologists should be available to augment what the ISS teacher can provide to individual students. They may be better equipped to serve or refer students to community services with trauma-informed therapeutic interventions. Hochman and Worner (1987) found group counseling as an ISS intervention "can increase students' self-esteem and their awareness of self-defeating attitudes and behaviors, help students set and follow through on personal goals, and contribute to building effective problem solving skills" (p. 93).

Change the Name of ISS. Last but not least, changing the name of ISS is essential. "Suspension" is an exclusionary term whether it occurs outside or inside the school. Shifting ISS from an exclusionary to inclusionary intervention warrants giving it a name that reflects teaching prosocial behavior and emphasizing discipline, not punishment. For example, the Focus and Recovery (FAR) Room is Taylor Middle's alternative to ISS (Fauquier County Public Schools). The FAR process is anchored to the schoolwide PBIS expectations and embeds restorative practices. Taylor Middle School was able to staff a full-time paraprofessional as the FAR Room teacher. A pass to the FAR Room is defined as a minor referral and can be issued for disrespect, disruption, or defiance; however, before a student is sent to the FAR Room, the teacher must document with an administrator at least three interventions. Those interventions could be a redirection, a quiet conversation with the student, and a short time away from the task to provide the student with an opportunity to refocus. Once a teacher has tried at least three interventions with little impact on student behavior and the teacher identifies the need for some space, the teacher can send the student to the FAR Room. When the student receives the pass, the teacher is asked to complete a brief form to inform the FAR Room teacher about the circumstances (see Figure 6.9).

Once the student arrives, the FAR Room teacher gives the student an opportunity to de-escalate if needed, and then the student must answer a set of restorative questions. There are two sets of restorative questions they use to facilitate reflection (Figure 6.9). After the students have answered the questions, the FAR Room teacher prepares them to have a restorative chat with the classroom teacher who sent them to FAR Room. This chat will occur during homeroom the following school day. Students who are sent to the FAR room are released at the end of the class period to continue on with the day. The FAR Room teacher enters the data into the SWIS database and informs each student's homeroom teacher where the student needs to go in the morning to complete the restorative chat. If the student does not answer the questions and is not ready to return to the class where they had the issue, they return to the FAR Room to provide more time to process. Trained teacher leaders and administrators are available to facilitate restorative chats if necessary.

Restorative Questionnaire I is used when there is a need to respond to challenging behavior

1. What happened?
2. What were you thinking at the time?
3. What have you thought about since?
4. Who has been affected by what you have done?
5. What do you think you need to do to make things right?

Restorative Questionnaire II is used when a student has been harmed by another person

1. What did you think when you realized what happened?
2. What impact has this incident had on you and others?
3. What has been the hardest thing for you?
4. What do you think needs to happen to make things right?

Figure 6.9 Focus and Recovery (FAR) Room Questions for the student... (personal communication, J. Linthicum, 2018)

Resources to Respond

We selected the resources below based on research and feedback from practitioners. This list is not exhaustive, rather a starting point for educators interested in developing trauma-responsiveness in their schools by *empowering others to act* and *generating quick wins*.

Title	Type	Description	QR Code/Link	Link
CASEL	WEBSITE	The Collaborative for Academic, Social, and Emotional Learning provides recommendations about research-based SEL practices.		https://tiresources.pub/38
Caring Schools Community	SEL CURRICULUM	Evidence-based SEL curriculum designed for students in Kindergarten through 8th Grade.		https://tiresources.pub/39
Second Step Curriculum	SEL CURRICULUM	Easy to use lesson plans and activities designed to support SEL in Pre-Kindergarten through 8th Grade.		https://tiresources.pub/40
MindUP	SEL CURRICULUM	Low cost SEL curriculum for Pre-Kindergarten through 8th Grade.		https://tiresources.pub/41
Sanford Harmony	SEL CURRICULUM	Free SEL curriculum for Pre-Kindergarten through 6th Grade.		https://tiresources.pub/42
Suite360	SEL CURRICULUM	Standards-based online programs designed to provide schools with a consistent SEL curriculum in Kindergarten through 12th Grade.		https://tiresources.pub/43
RULER: Emotional Intelligence	WEBSITE	Use the power of emotions to create a more effective and compassionate society through a systemic approach to SEL.		https://tiresources.pub/44
Flamboyan Foundation	WEBSITE	Provides resources to combat inequity in schools by focusing on increasing family engagement.		https://tiresources.pub/63
The ZONE	VIDEO	A secondary example of an alternative to in-school suspension.		https://tiresources.pub/46
Fix School Discipline	BOOK	A toolkit designed to support school-wide discipline; including trauma-sensitive strategies.		https://tiresources.pub/47

Figure 6.10 Resources to Respond

Title	Type	Description	QR Code/Link	Link
Conscious Discipline	WEBSITE	Acquire the strategies necessary to create a positive learning environment to increase student achievement.		https://tiresources.pub/48
PBIS	WEBSITE	A wealth of resources designed to improve social, emotional, and academic outcomes for all students. The Tiered Fidelity Inventory (TFI) can be found here.		https://tiresources.pub/49
Zones of Regulation	FRAMEWORK	A framework designed to help students express their emotions and learn how to self-regulate.		https://tiresources.pub/50
The Mandt System	TRAINING	Assists with understanding trauma and provides certification in de-escalation techniques.		https://tiresources.pub/51
Professional Quality of Life Scale	QUESTIONNAIRE	The ProQOL is the most commonly used measure of the negative and positive affects of helping others who experience suffering and trauma.		https://tiresources.pub/52
Holistic Life Foundations	WEBSITE	Nonprofit in Baltimore dedicated to yoga, mindfulness, and self-care for students.		https://tiresources.pub/53
Edutopia: How Learning Happens	VIDEO	A series of videos highlighting how schools can align practices with the scientific explanation of how learning occurs.		https://tiresources.pub/54
Community & Family Engagement	REFERENCE DOCUMENT	Principals share how to build a strong school community.		https://tiresources.pub/55
Circle Forward	BOOK	Assists teachers with implementing restorative circles with students in classrooms.		https://tiresources.pub/56
Missouri PBIS Support	WEBSITE	Comprehensive resources created to support schools and divisions with the development of tiered supports.		https://tiresources.pub/57

Figure 6.10 Continued

References

Algozzine, B., Barrett, S., Eber, L., George, H., Horner, R., Lewis, T., … & Sugai, G. (2014). *School-wide PBIS tiered fidelity inventory*. OSEP Technical Assistance Center on Positive Behavioral Interventions and Supports. Retrieved from www.pbis.org.

Anderson, E., Blitz, L., & Saastamoinen, M. (2015). Exploring a school-university model for professional development with classroom staff: Teaching trauma-informed approaches. *School Community Journal, 25*(2), 113–134.

Ashdown, D., & Bernard, M. (2012). Can explicit instruction in social and emotional learning skills benefit the social-emotional development, well-being, and academic achievement of young children? *Early Childhood Education Journal, 39*(6), 397–405. doi: 10.1007/s10643-011-0481-x.

Bailey, B. (2018a). Seven powers for conscious adults. *Conscious Discipline.* Retrieved from https://consciousdiscipline.com/methodology/seven-powers/.

Bailey, B. (2018b). Seven skills of discipline. *Conscious Discipline.* Retrieved from https://consciousdiscipline.com/methodology/seven-skills/10.1016/j.biopsych .2017.08.023.

Bradshaw, C. P., Mitchell, M. M., O'Brennan, L. M., & Leaf, P. J. (2010). Multilevel exploration of factors contributing to the overrepresentation of black students in office disciplinary referrals. *Journal of Educational Psychology, 102*(2), 508-520. doi: doi.org/10.1037/a0018450.

Byrd, C. M. (2016, September). Does culturally relevant teaching work? An examination from student perspectives. *SAGE Open, 6*(3), 1–10. doi: 10.1177/2158244016660744.

Center for Restorative Process. (2018). Retrieved from http://www.centerforresto rativeprocess.com/restorative-justice-and-restorative-practices.html.

Collaborative for Academic, Social, and Emotional Learning. (2018). Retrieved from https://casel.org/.

Davidson, R. J. (2018). *Meet Richard Davidson, Founder of the Center for Healthy Minds* [Video]. Retrieved from https://www.richardjdavidson.com/.

Delisio, E. R. (2007). Evaluating in-school suspension programs. *Education World.* Retrieved from https://www.educationworld.com/a_issues/chat/chat082.shtml.

Dickinson, M. C., & Miller, T. L. (2006, Fall). Issues regarding in-school suspensions and high school students with disabilities. *American Secondary Education, 35*(1), 72-83.

Downey, J. A. (2008). Recommendations for fostering educational resilience in the classroom. *Preventing School Failure: Alternative Education for Children and Youth (53)*1, 56-64. https://doi.org/10.3200/PSFL.53.1.56-64.

Edwards, L. (2016). Homogeneity and inequality: School discipline inequality and the role of racial composition. *Social Forces, 95*(1), 55–75. doi: 10.1093/sf/ sow038.

Fairbanks, S., Sugai, G., Guardino, D., & Lathrop, M. (2007). Response to intervention: Examining classroom behavior support in second grade. *Exceptional Children, 73*(3), 288–310.

Forbes, H. T. (2012). *Help for Billy: A beyond consequences approach to helping challenging children in the classroom.* Boulder, CO: Beyond Consequences Institute, LLC.

Gonzalez, S. (2012, May 4). In school-suspension: A better alternative or waste of time? *State Impact.* Retrieved from https://stateimpact.npr.org/florida/2012/05/0 4/floridas-in-school-suspension-policy-keeps-students-out-of-class/.

Gootman, M. E. (1998). Effective in-house suspension. *Educational Leadership, 56*(1), 39–41.

Gorski, P. (2014, April 10). Imagining equity literacy. *Teaching Tolerance.* Retrieved from https://www.tolerance.org/magazine/imagining-equity-literacy.

Hochman, S., & Worner, W. (1987). In-school suspension and group counseling: Helping the at-risk student. *NASSP Bulletin 65*(441), 93–96. doi: 10.1177/019263658707150124.

In-school suspension: A learning tool. (2018). *Education World.* Retrieved from https://www.educationworld.com/a_admin/admin/admin329.shtml.

Joyce, B. R., & Showers, B. (2002). *Student achievement through staff development,* 3rd ed. Alexandria, VA: ASCD.

Kotter, J. P. (2012). *Leading change.* Boston, MA: Harvard Business School Press.

Lewis, T. (2013). *Myths, misunderstandings, and milestones in implementing school-wide positive behavior support.* Presentation, Columbia, MO.

Mayworm, A., & Sharkey, J. (2014). Ethical considerations in a three-tiered approach to school discipline policy and practice. *Psychology in the Schools, 51*(7), 693–704. doi: 10.1002/pits.21782.

McIntosh, K. (2017). Strategies for neutralizing implicit bias in school discipline. Retrieved from http://pbisconference.org/files/2017/04/McIntosh-Implicit-Bias-2017-4-24.pdf.

McIntosh, K., & Goodman, S. (2016). *Integrated multi-tiered systems of support: Blending RTI and PBIS.* New York: Guilford Press.

Meyers, D. (2018, June). *Home is where the relationship begins: Home visitation as a family engagement strategy* [PowerPoint slides]. Trauma-Informed Schools Conference, St. Charles, MO.

Minch, D. (2019). *Engaging families in VTSS: Moving forward to meaningful partnerships.* Tampa, FL: University of South Florida.

Missouri Department of Mental Health and Partners. (2014). Missouri model: A developmental framework for trauma informed approaches. Retrieved from https://dmh.mo.gov/trauma/MO%20Model%20Working%20Document%20february%202015.pdf.

Morris, R. C., & Howard, A. C. (2003). Designing an effective in-school suspension program. *Clearing House, 76*(3), 156–159. doi: 10.1080/00098650309601994.

Morrow, G. (1987). *The compassionate school: A practical guide to educating abused and traumatized children.* Upper Saddle River, NJ: Prentice Hall.

National Child Traumatic Stress Network, Schools Committee. (2017). *Creating, supporting, and sustaining trauma-informed schools: A system framework.* Los Angeles, CA: National Center for Child Traumatic Stress.

National Education Association. (2018). Why cultural competence? To help educators close achievement gaps. Retrieved from http://www.nea.org/home/39783.htm.

Nixon, J., & Keels, M. (2018, April). *Improving school-wide culture and climate through social and emotional learning.* Practice Brief #6. TREP Project. Retrieved from http://docs.wixstatic.com/ugd/fc6e9a_6fb14ab4dfbc4a92a9fa440fecbc2233.pdf.

Payne, R. K. (2018). *Emotional poverty in all demographics.* Highlands, TX: Aha! Process, Inc.

Payne, A. A., & Welch, K. (2015). Restorative justice in schools: The influence of race on restorative discipline. *Youth & Society, 47*(4), 539-564. doi: 10.1177/0044118X12473125.

Peterson, R., Miller, C., & Skiba, R. (2004). A framework for planning safe and responsive schools. *Beyond Behavior*, *13*(3), 12–16.

Pierson, R. (2013, May 3). *Rita Pierson: Every kid needs a champion* [Video file]. Retrieved from https://www.youtube.com/watch?v=SFnMTHhKdkw.

Purtle, J. (2018). Systematic review of evaluations of trauma-informed organizational-interventions that include staff trainings. *Trauma, Violence, & Abuse*, *21*(4), 1–16. doi: 10.1177/1524838018791304.

Positive Behavioral Interventions & Supports. (2018). Retrieved from https://www.pbis.org/.

Romero, V. E., Robertson, R., & Warner, A. (2018). *Building resilience in students impacted by adverse childhood experiences: A whole-staff approach.* Thousand Oaks, CA: Corwin.

Rosen, A. (2018). Four reasons to start the day with morning meetings. Aperture Education. Retrieved from https://apertureed.com/sel-integration/4-reasons-start-school-day-morning-meetings/.

Ryan, J. B., Katsiyannis, A., Peterson, R., & Chmelar, R. (2007). IDEA 2004 and disciplining students with disabilities. *NASSP Bulletin*, *91*(2), 130–140. doi: 10.1177/0192636507302309

Safe and Responsive Schools. (2018). Retrieved from https://k12engagement.unl.edu/the-safe-and-responsive-schools-project.

Sheets, J. (1996). Designing an effective in-school suspension program to change student behavior. *NASSP Bulletin*, *80*(579), 86–90. doi: 10.1177/019263659608057915.

Short, P. M. (1988). Planning and developing in-school suspension programs. *Monographs in Education*, *9*. Retrieved from https://files.eric.ed.gov/fulltext/ED303875.pdf.

Siegel, D. (2012). Dr. Dan Siegel presenting a hand model of the brain. Retrieved from https://www.youtube.com/watch?v=gm9CIJ74Oxw.

Steinberg, M., & Lacoe, J. (2017). What do we know about school discipline reform? Assessing the alternatives to suspensions and expulsions. *Education Next*, *17*(1), 44-52.

Stewart, K. (2016). Can restorative practices help to reduce disparities in school discipline data?: A review of the literature. *Multicultural Perspectives*, *18*(2), 97–102. doi: 10.1080/15210960.2016.1159099.

Substance Abuse and Mental Health Services Administration. (2014). *Guiding principles of trauma-informed care.* *22*(2). Retrieved from https://www.samhsa.gov/samhsaNewsLetter/Volume_22_Number_2/trauma_tip/guiding_principles.html.

Sullivan, D., & Tifft, L. (2001). *Restorative justice: Healing the foundations of our everyday lives.* Monsey, NY: Willow Tree Press Inc.

Sullivan, J. S. (1989). Elements of a successful in-school suspension program. *NASSP Bulletin*, *73*(516), 32–38. doi: 10.1177/019263658907351607.

Taylor, R. D., Oberle, E., Durlak, J. A., & Weissberg, R. P. (2017). Promoting positive youth development through school-based social and emotional learning interventions: A meta-analysis of follow-up effects. *Child Development*, *88*(4), 1156–1171. doi: 10.1111/cdev.12864.

US Department of Education. (2018). Every student succeeds act. Retrieved from https://www.ed.gov/essa?src=rn.

Vanderslice, R. (1999). Developing effective in-school suspension programs. *Delta Kappa Gamma Bulletin, 65*(4), 33–38.

Vavrus, F., & Cole, K. M. (2002, June). I didn't do nothin': The discursive construction of school suspension. *The Urban Review, 34*(2), 87–111. doi: 10.1023/A:1015375215801.

Virginia Department of Education. (2020). Virginia's 5Cs. Retrieved on October 9, 2020 from http://www.virginiaisforlearners.virginia.gov/media-library/.

Wachtel, T. (2009). *My three decades of using restorative practices with delinquent and at-risk youth: Theory, practice and research outcomes.* Bethlem, PA: International Institute for Restorative Practices.

Welsh, R. O., & Little, S. (2018, October). The school discipline dilemma: A comprehensive review of disparities and alternative approaches. *Review of Educational Research, 88*(5), 752–794. doi: 10.3102/0034654318791582.

Yang, C., Bear, G., & May, H. (2018). Multilevel associations between school-wide social-emotional learning approach and student engagement across elementary, middle, and high schools. *School Psychology Review, 47*(1), 45–61. doi: 10.17105/SPR-2017-0003.V47-1.

Zhang, D., Katsiyannis, A., & Herbst, M. (2004). Disciplinary exclusions in special education: A 4-year analysis. *Behavioral Disorders, 29*(4), 337–347. Retrieved from http://www.jstor.org.proxy.library.vcu.edu/stable/23889526.

7 Resist

Avoiding Retraumatization through Trauma-Informed Systems and Supports

Having developed a trauma-responsive staff and more resilient students, the final mission is to **R**esist retraumatization. Retraumatization is any situation or environment that resembles an individual's trauma literally or symbolically, and/or triggers difficult feelings and reactions associated with the original trauma (University of Buffalo, 2019). Exclusionary discipline is often such a trigger. The more student discipline is intentionally aligned with trauma-informed principles, the less likely retraumatization is to occur. To *sustain the momentum of change* and *establish systems and supports* (Kotter, 2012), there must be an institutional commitment to normalizing policies, procedures, staffing, evaluation, and funding of a trauma-informed organization. According to the Missouri Model:

> *Trauma-Informed* organizations have made trauma-responsive practices the organizational norm. In these organizations, trauma-responsive practices have become so accepted and so thoroughly embedded that implementation no longer depends on a few leaders. The organization works with other partners to strengthen collaboration around being trauma-informed.
>
> (Missouri Department of Mental Health and Partners, 2014, p. 5)

Other indicators of being trauma-informed include the following:

- School leaders demonstrate a commitment to trauma-informed principles.
- People outside the agency understand the organization's mission to be trauma-informed.
- The organization uses data to inform decision-making at all levels.

- Ongoing professional development on school initiatives is available to new and existing staff.
- Ongoing coaching is available to staff on-site and in real time by trauma-informed experts.
- Funds are allocated to support trauma-informed practices. (Missouri Department of Mental Health and Partners, 2014, p. 15)

All of these efforts take time and intentionality. The guiding coalition should return to Appendix D and support each strategic vision statement with details of professional development, organizational structure, staffing, community partnerships, and a timeline of implementation.

Figure 7.1 Discipline Reform Model: RESIST (Kotter, 2012; Missouri Department of Mental Health and Partners, 2014; Substance Abuse and Mental Health Services Administration, 2014)

Role of the Principal

To sustain the momentum of change and establish systems and supports, the principal must emphasize accountability. Principal *Joshua Cole* shared that his school experienced a high rate of turnover during his first few years, and he was comfortable with people leaving. He hired and retained staff at Ecoff Elementary, Chesterfield County Public Schools, who were willing participants and committed learners as the school implemented trauma-responsive practices. Cole referenced *Good to Great* by Jim Collins who writes that successful leaders get the right people on the bus. "A culture of discipline is not just about action. It is about getting disciplined people who engage in disciplined thought and who then take disciplined action" (2001, p. 143). To develop student discipline, adults must model expectations. Personal accountability is essential to implement trauma-responsive practices with fidelity.

Stories of Systematization

This chapter outlines how several Virginia school divisions are systematically Resisting re-traumatization, integrating practices, staffing, and addressing the needs of every child. These systems have decreased suspensions and racial disproportionality of student discipline. All practitioners interviewed used multi-tiered systems of supports (MTSS) for organizing academic, behavioral, and social-emotional learning. Stories from these divisions provide models of equity that have sustained the momentum of change. These models also demonstrate that the process of becoming a trauma-informed school or division depends ultimately on strong leadership.

Virginia Tiered Systems of Support (VTSS) Resist

Virginia Tiered Systems of Supports (VTSS) is a state model of an MTSS that aligns academic, behavioral, and mental health supports with an explicit focus on measurable growth. Currently, 60 divisions in Virginia are

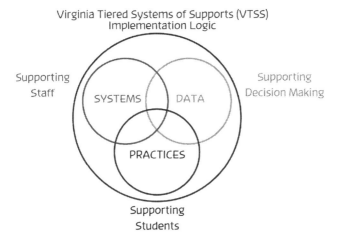

Figure 7.2 Virginia Tiered Systems of Supports (VTSS) Implementation Logic (Virginia Tiered Systems of Supports, 2020)

participating in VTSS (VTSS, 2020). Virginia Tiered Systems of Supports divisions have consistently reduced the number of general education and special education students who receive exclusionary discipline (Saimre, 2018). Additionally, 94% of VTSS divisions have demonstrated consistent growth for student performance on state assessments in English; 75% of VTSS divisions have demonstrated consistent growth on the state assessments in Math (Saimre, 2018). During the 2016–2017 school year, the graduate rate in VTSS divisions was 1.38% higher than the state average. Between the 2015–2016 and 2016–2017 school years, the most updated data available, VTSS divisions had a 10% decrease in the disproportionate number of Black students receiving short-term suspensions (Saimre, 2018).

Patrick Farrell, behavior support specialist, Charlottesville City Schools, worked with the VTSS Division Level Team (DLT) to develop a framework for all factors impacting students. Farrell and the DLT divided the Tier I areas of focus into five components: Core Instruction/Literacy, Core Instruction/Math, Behavior, Mental Wellness, and Attendance. Farrell explained, "[The division] is not only building those systems of support for kids, but for the adults as well."

Developing an MTSS requires progress monitoring at all three tiers and across domains (academics, behavior, and mental health). Farrell emphasized, "A big piece for us is integration. People don't need one more thing in their headspace. We've been very intentional on how our training works

	Core Instruction Literacy	Core Instruction Math	Behavior	Mental Wellness	Attendance
Defined	ALL students will receive differentiated core instruction.	ALL students will receive differentiated core instruction.	ALL students will receive differentiated core instruction.	ALL students will receive differentiated core instruction.	ALL students whose good attendance could be maintained and cultivated as long as the universal, prevention oriented supports are in place.
Curriculum & Instruction	See the CCS GOS and CCS Literacy Foundations document	See the CCS GPS	See School-Based Tier 1 PBIS Plan	CASEL Five SEL Competencies; Barking Dog; Second Step; MindUP; SchoolConnect; Youth Mental Health First Aid	Attendance Works Tier 1 Strategies

Figure 7.3 Charlottesville City Schools (CCS) Tier 1 Core Instruction (personal communication, P. Farrell, 2018)

within the framework of VTSS. [Our teachers] talk in the language of tiered systems."

Farrell focused on supporting teacher efficacy by empowering them to create classroom communities. With fewer discipline referrals, principals have more time to be instructional leaders. Farrell devoted time to pursuing community partnerships, writing grants, and getting creative with funding. He said partnering with trauma-informed experts is critical "to make sure that you're really going the right way." Hiring new teachers who are dedicated to developing relationships with students is also a priority. "The founding component of every single great trauma-responsive program is connecting to an adult."

The school divisions highlighted in this chapter are all VTSS divisions. They receive grant funds annually to support travel to professional learning events and materials needed to support ongoing implementation of tiered practices.

Fauquier County Public Schools (FCPS) Resists

Fauquier County Public Schools (FCPS) have been making progress with initiatives to support students with proactive, positive, and restorative practice. In 2014, FCPS received $100,000 from the federal Project AWARE grant to provide Youth Mental Health First Aid (YMHFA) training to 1,000 people throughout the county. The YMHFA training was offered free of charge to anyone interested. Law enforcement, healthcare professionals, educators, parents, and other community members participated. As of December 2018, over 1,400 people have been trained, including 400 FCPS employees. Trained school employees wear purple lanyards and have small signs in their classroom windows to let students know they are available if needed.

Resisting Stigma. The Mental Health and Schools Coalition has been working to **R**esist stigma about mental illness by educating community members with the YMHFA training and integrating unique services from outside providers into the schools. The Mental Health Association of Fauquier County (MHAFC) has created a searchable database on their website to help community members search for mental health providers (https://fauquier-mha.org/). *Sallie Morgan*, executive director of the MHAFC, is eager to shift the focus of the next bi-annual community forum to a youth community forum. There is a true sense of collaboration and collective efficacy amongst the members of the Mental Health and Schools Coalition and FCPS teachers and staff. The partnership has been instrumental in transforming the division into a trauma-informed model for others to emulate.

Resisting Substance Abuse. Morgan worked with *John Waldeck*, the former director of clinical services at the local Community Services Board and now special projects coordinator at MHAFC, to identify a community goal around **R**esisting substance abuse. Morgan shared:

> When John [Waldeck] and I became connected to the MHAFC in 2011, national data indicated 50% of mental health concerns show up by the age of 14 and 75% show up by the age of 24, so the MHAFC decided to focus on that age bracket to make the biggest difference with prevention.

In 2015, the MHSC received grant funds from the PATH Foundation, a local organization dedicated to providing grants to enhance the health and vitality of Fauquier, Rappahannock, and Culpeper Counties. The grant provided funding to re-administer the PRIDE Survey to all 7 through 12th graders in FCPS to gather longitudinal data on drug use to inform their action steps. The second administration of the PRIDE Survey revealed the average age of first use of substances in Fauquier County is 13. The Mental Health and Schools Coalition decided to begin putting interventions in place for fourth and fifth graders in an effort to prevent or delay first-time substance abuse.

Honore Hastings, executive director, Verdun Adventure Bound, is a member of the MHSC. Verdun Adventure Bound is a 55-acre wilderness retreat designed to provide outdoor experiences for groups of all types and ages. During the 2018–2019 school year, one elementary school from Fauquier County partnered with Verdun to provide the fourth and fifth grade students with monthly lessons during physical education classes at the school. *Sean McElhinney*, challenge course manager and lead facilitator, uses the Botvin LifeSkills Training curriculum to guide instruction and supplement the content with interactive activities (see Resources).

> We talk about self-esteem, decision-making, and standing up to peer pressure. We use the Botvin strategy "Stop, Think, Go", stop before you make a decision, think about the consequences, and make a decision. Each one of the topics we discuss, we discuss it briefly and play a quick game to make the concept come alive for the kids.

The partnership between Verdun and FCPS has provided students with unique experiences and has modeled ways for them to handle challenging social situations and avoid substance use. Service providers across the community who have participated in the MHSC are all working toward the same goals and each organization fulfills a specific need. They view themselves as partners versus competitors. *Carolyn Lamm*, supervisor of student support services shared:

> As a part of the coalition, we worked collaboratively with the school principal, the school counselor, Kathleen from CADRE (Community

Alliance for Drug Rehabilitation and Education), and Honore from Verdun to come up with all these plans. A big goal for us is to build capacity for our folks so it won't just be these people coming in doing fun activities and going away and our teachers never learning anything about how to make the lessons more engaging, impactful, and experiential. So the teachers are pairing with outside providers during lessons so we aren't just providing a service for the students, we are providing change in practices for the adult educators in the building.

Henrico County Public Schools (HCPS) Resists

Nyah Hamlett, assistant superintendent for instructional support, explained that Henrico County Public Schools (HCPS) remain concerned about the 2% of students who have had two or more out-of-school suspensions. These are the students who are most in need of uninterrupted education. Of particular concern are suspensions of Black students and SWD, which have actually increased over time.

Therapeutic Supports. Hamlett is advocating for a broader range of options in programming on the continuum of specialized services for SWD, especially therapeutic supports for Tier 3 interventions. Tier 3 interventions at each school appear different, depending on student age and resource availability. HCPS is building capacity with trauma-informed personnel, such as school psychologists, counselors, or other mental health specialists. HCPS created Behavior Learning Intervention Support Services (BLISS) programs for students with disabilities whose behaviors are trauma related. Teachers in the BLISS program receive trauma-informed training specific to behavior management. They are each designated as a *critical response teacher* (CRT). They provide both pull-out and push-in instructional services, as well as consultative behavior supports and strategies in the collaborative classroom. Students with significant needs for behavior support can be placed at BLISS schools division-wide through the IEP process. One goal of the BLISS program is to offset a high number of private therapeutic day treatment placements county-wide and to build student resilience and self-regulation.

New Support Positions. Hamlett has overseen the creation and hiring of new student support positions. In 2015, HCPS created a position in the Office of Student Support and Disciplinary Review. The job description of the *coordinator of behavior supports* includes the following essential duties:

- Support and prove feedback and professional development to all behavior support staff and interventionists, ISS Coordinators, Deans of Student Support and Discipline, and mentoring programs.
- Coordinate district-wide PBIS training and coaching.

- Collaborate with the Preventive Services Specialist to assess and provide supports for African American male students, such as cultural proficiency training.
- Conduct research and provide technical assistance on understanding the school-to-prison pipeline.
- Develop equitable strategies to assess and address disproportionate discipline and alternatives to OSS.
- Monitor students who have been long term suspended or expelled by visiting them at alternative placement sites and assisting with transition plans back to the comprehensive school. (HCPS, 2016, para. 2)

In 12 secondary schools with relatively high rates of ODRs and disproportionality, HCPS has hired a *dean of student support and discipline*. In five elementary schools, HCPS has designated a *positive behavior support teacher*. These two positions require a similar skillset:

The individual should have the ability to develop and implement positive behavior supports. Knowledge of [childhood or adolescent] social-emotional development, including an understanding of mental health diagnoses and trauma and how this impacts academic performance. The ability to develop and use techniques for dealing with youth who exhibit inappropriate behavior. The candidate should have the ability to develop effective behavioral intervention plans and prove direct behavioral interventions in a school setting. The ability to build relationships and work with a diverse group of individuals from a variety of socio-economic and cultural backgrounds.

(HCPS, 2016, para. 3)

When students are suspended or sent to an alternative school intervention, the dean of students also provides re-entry meetings with the student and parent upon their return to the comprehensive school setting. According to *William Noel, Sr.*, director of disciplinary review,

They are not always met with open arms and a clean slate. We want them to have some sort of help when they get back. [They need to be] linked with someone, at least one adult in that building, who they feel comfortable going to if things start to go awry.

Another position, *clinical school-based mental health supervisor*, was created in HCPS to coordinate all aspects of school-based mental health counseling and therapy, administer and provide trauma-informed clinical support to schools, coordinate the HCPS Trauma-Informed Schools Task Force, and lead the HCPS Crisis Intervention Team together with the directors of psychological supports, counseling, and social work. To meet increasing needs among younger students, HCPS aims to hire an additional 42 elementary counselors so that every building has two counselors.

Revision of the Code of Conduct. As changes to policy, support services, and staffing were taking place in HCPS, a logical next step was to review discipline procedures. Hamlett and Noel worked together to oversee the revision of the *HCPS Code of Student Conduct.* According to Noel, the Code's recommended consequences for the same violation "had ranged from a conference with the student all the way down to recommendation for expulsion." Actual consequences had ranged widely among principals. To eliminate the disparity:

> We wanted to make it more supportive with interventions rather than having suspensions and expulsion be the first go-to. We wanted to put things in *The Code* that would make it supportive and have things in place before we have to suspend, and before we even have to remove a child from the classroom.

It took two years for the five magisterial districts of HCPS to adopt the new *Code of Student Conduct.* The Code (HCPS, 2018) now provides five Code Violation Categories that are aligned with interventions and responses as an MTSS. Category 1 (Tier 1) violations suggest classroom and student support team interventions up to in-school suspension, called *Reset.* Category 2 (Tier 2) violations include Reset with restorative practices up to a maximum three-day out-of-school suspensions (OSS). Category 3 (Tier 3) violations include a maximum five-day OSS. Category 4 (Tier 3) violations include a maximum 10-day OSS. Category 5 (Tier 3) include a possible long term suspension (up to 45 days) or expulsion, and probable placement at an alternate educational environment. The *Code* also outlines the rights and responsibilities of students, parents/guardians, and HCPS employees.

In 2017, the *Code* was recognized by the National School Boards Association as one of five large school systems in the US to receive a first-place honor in the 2017 Magna Awards for taking bold and innovative steps to improve the lives of students and their communities. Since its adoption, HCPS's revised *Code of Student Conduct* has resulted in a significant reduction of exclusionary discipline (see Figure 7.4). Noel is proud of the results. In 2017–2018, "94% of our students had no out-of-school suspensions, 4% had at least one out-of-school suspension, and 2% had at least two out-of-school suspensions." By January 2019, zero students had been expelled without some form of alternative education service, "and we still have not had a student who's come close to 45 days out of school with no service. Each of those who are long term suspended have received some form of instructional programming or support."

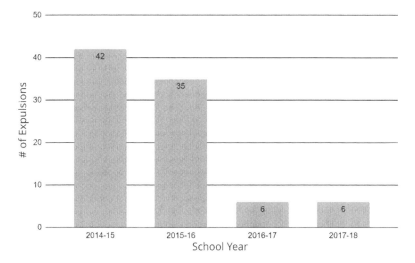

Figure 7.4 Henrico County Public Schools HCPS Expulsion Data (HCPS, 2018)

A Focus on Equity. Henrico's *Code of Student Conduct* has served as a model for other divisions and for revisions of Virginia's state code of conduct. Yet, even with significant reduction in overall expulsions and suspensions, Noel remains concerned about disproportionality.

> So it won us that award, but when you break those numbers down, of that 2% who had two or more out-of-school suspensions, over 80% are African-American, 13.7% are Caucasian, and 5.3% other. We're reducing the overall suspensions, but the gap still remains.

To address this gap, poverty has become the focus of HCPS systems of support. Hamlett used discipline data to map which schools in the division had the most students with three or more suspensions. She found that the vast majority of these students attended schools with over 75% free and reduced lunch rates, and 77% of these students were Black. Trauma-informed personnel, programs, and professional development have thus been designated to these schools through the Department of Equity, Diversity, and Opportunity. This department is providing training to teachers and administrators in restorative practices and culturally responsive education, and is charged "to empower families by successfully bridging gaps and building connections among families, schools and communities" (HCPS, 2019). The department, funded by Title I grants, oversees 21 schools and 26 preschool programs with Title I staff. The department organizes division-wide parent information and education sessions through the Family and Educator Resource Center (FERC). In addition to a permanent office, the FERC has a mobile outreach called *The Big Blue Bus*, which travels to neighborhood communities to meet families where they live. According to Hamlett, "We really push some of our efforts with family engagement in those areas so we can try to engage families and have a better understanding of the population which we serve beyond skin color."

Loudoun County Public Schools (LCPS) Resists

To streamline mental health services across tiers of supports, Loudoun County Public Schools (LCPS) developed a universal implementation inventory of its mental health framework and consolidated supports into an MTSS Office. The MTSS Office oversees all interventions for behavior, academics, and mental health from an integrated whole child lens. By restructuring its services, LCPS more effectively manages mental health supports at all three tiers. Figure 7.5 is the LCPS Mental Health Framework at the secondary level.

Unified Mental Health Teams. To maintain fidelity of implementation of all student supports at the secondary level, Superintendent *Eric Williams* initiated site-based and community-supported structures called Unified

Tier	Behavior	Bullying/ Violence	Social Emotional	Suicide Prevention	Substance Abuse
Intensive Tier 3	FBA & BIP / Technical MANDT / Restorative Conference / Collaborative Problem-solving	Individual Counseling / Threat Assessment / Safety Plan / Restorative Conference	Individual Counseling / School Within a School / Wrap Around/MDT / Student Referral & Assessment	Suicide Screening Referral & Follow-up	3-Day Insight Program and Assessment / Individual Support / Student Referral & Assessment Program
Targeted Tier 2	Check In - Check Out / Informal Behavior Plan / Relational MANDT / Restorative Circles	Group Counseling / Threat Assessment / Violence Risk Reduction Groups	Group Counseling / Classroom Skill Instruction / Restorative Circles	Group and Individual Counseling	Alcohol & Substance Prevention Groups / Tobacco Education Program
Universal Tier 1	PBIS / Restorative Practice Langauge and Community Circles	Stop-Walk-Talk Expect Respect	Sources of Strength / PEER / Classroom Guidance / Restorative Language and Community Circles	SOS Signs of Suicide / SOS Signs of Suicide Second Act / SOS Training Trusted Adults	Substance Use Prevention Education / PEER

Figure 7.5 Loudoun County Public Schools (LCPS) Mental Health Framework (LCPS, 2018)

Mental Health Teams (UMHTs). Every middle and high school in LCPS has a school psychologist and social worker. They meet once a month with all of the counselors, administrators, student assistant specialists, and school nurses to review interventions at each tier of support. At Tier 2 and Tier 3, they analyze data and identify what resources they need at the problem-solving and monitoring levels of crisis support. At Tier 1, they look at how they are communicating to all students and parents and assessing universal features for mental health within their buildings. Figure 7.6 illustrates middle and high school UMHTs. The division is now developing UMHTs at the elementary level.

Community Engagement. In an effort to increase community outreach, LCPS has invited parents and mental health providers to collaboratively address student mental health needs, including childhood trauma. The universal inventory includes measures of community outreach at the division and school levels. Parent education, for example, has included an evening series of approximately 10 events per year based on parent questions regarding mental health. The LCPS Parent Resource Center has helped to organize these seminars with expert speakers who are staff or local mental health providers, as well as with national trauma-informed experts. Topics have included anxiety, bullying, suicide prevention, restorative practices, and resilience.

Jennifer Wall, supervisor of student assistance specialists, has coordinated an annual mental health and wellness conference in partnership with Inova Health System, Loudoun County Mental Health, Substance Abuse and Developmental Services, and the local Community Services Board.

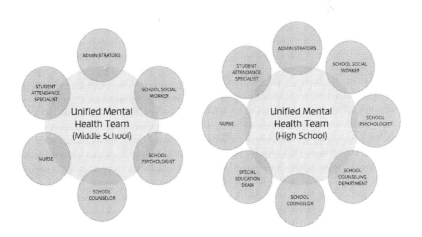

Figure 7.6 Loudoun County Public Schools (LCPS) Secondary Unified Mental Health Teams (LCPS, 2018)

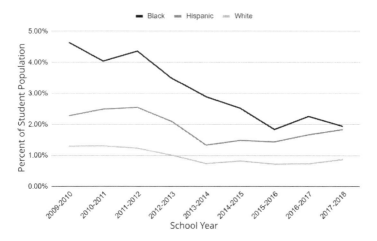

Figure 7.7 Loudoun County Public Schools (LCPS) Reduction of Suspension by Race/Ethnicity (LCPS, 2018)

The conferences have included keynote speakers, approximately 24 breakout sessions, and vendors. One of the goals is to assist in defining and coordinating school and community based mental health supports. Loudoun County Public Schools also communicates and coordinates with Loudoun Stop Child Abuse Now (SCAN) and ACE Interface to train supervisors, coordinators, specialists, and staff in Trauma 101 and Trauma 201 modules.

Decreasing Exclusionary Discipline and Disproportionality. Loudoun County Public Schools is a leader in providing comprehensive, holistic supports to K-12 students. Division-wide implementation of PBIS through the MTSS office has established an equitable, procedural framework for systematizing innovative programs, such as restorative practices and *Sources of Strength*. These programs have reduced exclusionary discipline while increasing student resilience and wellness. Over time, combined efforts have significantly reduced disproportionality of exclusionary discipline by ethnic groups and for students with disabilities (Figure 7.7). Additionally, recent data shows LCPS has lower suspension rates and lower discrepancy of suspension rates for Black/White students and SWD/SWOD than other Northern Virginia divisions.

Richmond Public Schools (RPS) Resists

The partnership between Richmond Public Schools (RPS), Greater Richmond Stop Child Abuse Now (GR-SCAN), and other agencies is an exemplar of how to design a system to *Resist* retraumatization.

Building Community Partnerships. Margo Buchanan, RPS resiliency project coordinator and trauma-informed child and family therapist, emphasized the essential role school leaders play in connecting schools with trauma-informed experts. Engaged principals who believe that additional strategies are needed to support students impacted by trauma make their students much more successful in school.

During the 2019–2020 school year, RPS division leadership made a commitment to trauma-informed practices by integrating goals into the division's strategic plan. In October 2019, GR-SCAN facilitated its first face-to-face professional learning opportunity for all building level administrators across RPS. The division level Trauma-Informed Leadership Team (TILT) met monthly to stay on target with goals for implementing trauma-informed practices.

During the 2020–2021 school year, CARES Act funds were allocated to expand partnerships with community organizations providing mental health services to students and families. The TILT developed a tiered system to organize services. Greater Richmond Stop Child Abuse Now coordinates and delivers all professional development related to Tier 1 trauma-responsive practices for educators across RPS. The Tier 1 supports include coaching and modeling of trauma-responsive practices with an explicit focus on self-care strategies for teachers. Communities in Schools, a trauma-informed partner, provides Tier 2 services for students who require additional support to be successful. ChildSavers and Richmond Behavioral Health Authority coordinate efforts to provide individual Tier 3 supports. Richmond Behavioral Health has therapist stations at schools across RPS to provide easy access to mental health services for students and families.

As of October 2020, there were 26 Trauma-Informed Community Networks (TICNs) in Virginia. The Virginia Trauma-Informed Community Network (VA-TICN) provides opportunities for multi-sector collaborations to occur. School representation is a critical component to the multi-sector collaboration. Greater Richmond Stop Child Abuse Now recognized a need for school personnel to collaborate, and developed the Greater Richmond Trauma-Informed Schools Committee (GR-TISC). When schools closed in March 2020 due to Covid-19, the GR-TISC facilitated discussions about ways educators could support social-emotional wellness through virtual instruction. Discussions addressed how to create a sense of community in a virtual classroom, self-care for teachers, and how to support families with virtual learning.

Building Relationships with Parents. To systematize family engagement, some school leaders may utilize a tiered system to organize family communication structures. Tier 1 family engagement strategies include creating culturally responsive family outreach, setting school-wide goals related to family engagement, and identifying barriers to family engagement and working to remove those barriers (Romero, Robertson, & Warner, 2018). Family engagement for students who require Tier 2 or Tier 3 supports requires collaborative problem solving and increased communication. School personnel should communicate frequently with families about their child's progress and partner with families to determine how they can reinforce strategies taught at school, at home. In some cases, family members may request additional support which is a great opportunity for schools to refer families to community agencies and organizations (Romero, Robertson, & Warner, 2018).

Resources to Resist

We selected the resources below based on research and feedback from practitioners. This list is not exhaustive, rather a starting point for principals interested in becoming a trauma-informed school by *sustaining momentum* and *establishing systems and supports*.

Title	Type	Description	QR Code/Link	Link
A Nation at Hope	WEBSITE	Recommendations for how to best support students and families informed by national survey data.		https://tiresources.pub/58
Virginia Department of Education Model Code of Conduct	REFERENCE DOCUMENT	The Virginia Department of Education published a revised model code of conduct to inform divisions interested in decreasing exclusionary discipline practices.		https://tiresources.pub/59
HCPS Code of Student Conduct	REFERENCE DOCUMENT	Henrico County Public Schools' Code of Conduct was used to inform the development of VDOE's Model Code of Conduct.		https://tiresources.pub/66
US Department of Education's Dual Capacity Framework	VIDEO	Provides a framework for how to cultivate meaningful home-school partnerships.		https://tiresources.pub/60
Youth Mental Health First Aid Training	TRAINING	Training designed for adults working with adolescents experiencing mental health challenges.		https://tiresources.pub/61
Formed Families Forward	WEBSITE	Support for foster, kinship, and adoptive families of children with disabilities.		https://tiresources.pub/62
Botvin Life Skills Training	CURRICULUM	Evidence-based prevention programs for families, schools, and communities.		https://tiresources.pub/64

Figure 7.8 Resources to Resist

References

Collins, J. (2001). *Good to great: Why some companies make the leap...and others don't*. New York: HarperCollins Publishers, Inc.

Henrico County Public Schools. (2016, May). *Job description: Coordinator of behavior supports*. Richmond, VA.

Henrico County Public Schools. (2018). Code of student conduct, 2018–2019. Retrieved from http://henricoschools.us/pdf/Schools/CodeOfStudentConduct.pdf.

Henrico County Public Schools. (2019). Foundational learning and family engagement. Retrieved from https://henricoschools.us/foundational-learning-family-engagement/.

Kotter, J. P. (2012). *Leading change*. Boston, MA: Harvard Business School Press.

Loudoun County Public Schools (LCPS) (2018, October 5). *Positive behavioral interventions and supports*. Retrieved from https://www.lcps.org/Page/213

Missouri Department of Mental Health and Partners. (2014). *Missouri model: A developmental framework for trauma informed approaches*. Retrieved from https://dmh.mo.gov/trauma/MO%20Model%20Working%20Document%20february%202015.pdf.

Romero, V. E., Robertson, R., & Warner, A. (2018). *Building resilience in students impacted by adverse childhood experiences: A whole-staff approach*. Thousand Oaks, CA: Corwin.

Saimre, M. (2018). *Tier 1 forum*. Presented by Virginia Tiered System of Supports, Williamsburg, VA.

Substance Abuse and Mental Health Services Administration. (2014). *Guiding principles of trauma-informed care. 22*(2). Retrieved from https://www.samhsa.gov/samhsaNewsLetter/Volume_22_Number_2/trauma_tip/guiding_principles.html

University at Buffalo. (2019). What is trauma-informed care? Retrieved from http://socialwork.buffalo.edu/social-research/institutes-centers/institute-on-trauma-and-trauma-informed-care/what-is-trauma-informed-care.html.

Virginia Tiered Systems of Supports. (2020). Retrieved from https://vtss-ric.org/.

Epilogue
Tending to a Crisis in Education

Now is a more critical time than ever to solve the problems of exclusionary discipline, especially for Black children. "In the United States, data reveal that Black Americans have contracted and died from the COVID-19 pandemic at rates that double, and sometimes triple their representation across various states" (Slay, 2020). Black children are more likely to have suffered trauma from the stress of a family member having contracted or died from the disease. Black children may have also suffered more physiologically and psychologically by disproportionate parent unemployment, lack of access to health care, and poor nutrition (Slay, 2020).

Experts worry that accompanying family stress has also made Black children more at risk to neglect and abuse. "An NBC News analysis of data from 43 states and Washington, D.C., found that reports of abuse and neglect in April 2020 dropped by an average of 40.6 percent in each state from the levels reported in the same month of 2019" (Ingram, 2020, para. 2). According to this same data, teachers and school officials nationally account for one-fifth of reports to Child Protective Services (CPS). "The absence of reports, however, means there's no way to confirm a surge, despite alarming anecdotes from emergency rooms, pediatricians and hotlines" (Ingram, 2020, para. 3).

Educationally, the pandemic has intensified the achievement gap for Black children due to inequitable access to computers and the internet for virtual instruction, and by academic gains often lost during instructional gaps (Slay, 2020). Meanwhile, the pandemic has borne witness on television and in many Black children's neighborhoods to the killing of George Floyd and Jacob Blake, mass protests, racial hatred, looting, and violence. These events are most certainly ACEs. According to Dr. Harold S. Koplewicz, MD, President and Medical Director of the Child Mind Institute,

> The stress of the coronavirus crisis has already brought a feeling of hopelessness to American life—particularly for adolescents. This latest example of racial violence and division has not surprisingly resulted in aggression on our streets and in our national conversation. We must

engage, comfort and reassure our young people and offer them productive ways to channel their anger and frustration and most of all be
heard. (Koplewics, 2020, para. 2–3)

We hope the effects of the pandemic and nationwide protests against institutional racism will be catalysts for educational reform and healing. The publication of this book is timely to guide leaders both inside and outside of the
classroom to equitably **R**espond with a trauma-informed lens that builds student resilience. The figure below summarizes our collective steps to REFORM.

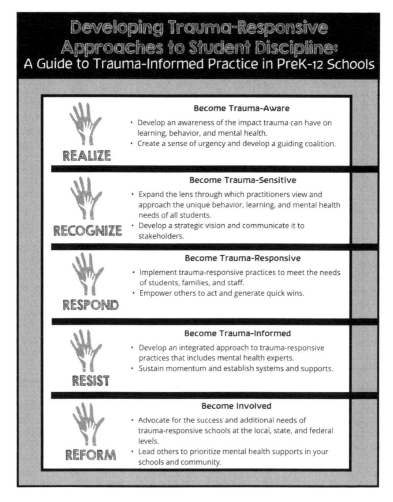

Figure E.1 Developing Trauma-Responsive Approaches to Student Disciplines: A
Guide to Trauma-Informed Practice in PreK-12 Schools (Kotter, 2012;
Missouri Department of Mental Health and Partners, 2014; Substance
Abuse and Mental Health Services Administration, 2014)

References

Ingram, J. (2020, July 26). Has child abuse surged under COVID-19? Despite alarming stories from ERs, there's no answer. *NBC News*. Retrieved from https://www.nbcnews.com/health/kids-health/has-child-abuse-surged-under-covid-19-despite-alarming-stories-n1234713.

Koplewics, H. S. (2020, June 1). Talking to kids about George Floyd. Child Mind Institute. Retrieved from https://childmind.org/blog/talking-to-kids-about-george-floyd/.

Slay, B. (2020, May 20). COVID-19 will intensify education inequities for Black students. Diverse: Issues in Higher Education. Retrieved from https://diverseeducation.com/article/177796/.

Appendix A
Realizing Trauma-Awareness

Rate your Guiding Coalition (School Leadership) and Staff: 1 = little or no realization; 2 = some realization; 3 = strong realization

1. School Leadership ____ Staff ____ realize that a trauma-aware definition of discipline is to train or develop by instruction and exercise especially in self-control and is not to punish or penalize for the sake of enforcing obedience and perfecting moral character.
2. School Leadership ____ Staff ____ realize that the primary focus of school discipline should be to support students vs. teachers.
3. School Leadership ____ Staff ____ realize that Black students, students with disabilities (SWD), and students who live in poverty are disproportionately suspended throughout the United States.
4. School Leadership ____ Staff ____ realize that that exclusionary discipline (e.g. office discipline referrals and suspensions) can often result in school avoidance, decreased academic achievement, increased behavior problems, increased likelihood of dropping out, substance abuse, involvement with juvenile justice systems, and/or retraumatization for students with childhood trauma.
5. School Leadership ____ Staff ____ realize that exclusionary discipline (e.g. office discipline referrals and suspensions) contributes to disproportionate achievement and discipline gaps especially for Black students, students with disabilities, and students living in poverty.
6. School Leadership ____ Staff ____ realize that exclusionary discipline (e.g. office discipline referrals and suspensions) contribute to the school-to-prison pipeline.
7. School Leadership ____ Staff ____ realize what implicit bias is and that exclusionary discipline (e.g. office discipline referrals and suspensions) are often the result of implicit bias.
8. School Leadership ____ Staff ____ realize poverty is an injustice that needs to be addressed structurally vs. individually (the *system* has a deficit, not the student).
9. School Leadership ____ Staff ____ realize and believe all students can learn and emotionally self-regulate with adult support and instruction.
10. School Leadership ____ Staff ____ realize that Adverse Childhood Experiences (ACEs) and chronic stress can have a traumatic impact on children's ability to emotionally self-regulate.
11. School Leadership ____ Staff ____ realize the brain science behind childhood trauma.
12. School Leadership ____ Staff ____ realize that every school has students who are impacted by ACES and trauma.
13. School Leadership ____ Staff ____ realize ACES and resulting trauma affect every age, race, gender, and socioeconomic level.
14. School Leadership ____ Staff ____ realize ACES and resulting trauma especially affect students living in poverty.
15. School Leadership ____ Staff ____ realize the prevalence and impact of ACES and childhood trauma.
16. School Leadership ____ Staff ____ realize all students cannot perform academically or pass standardized tests if they are not emotionally self-regulated.
17. School Leadership ____ Staff ____ realize that trauma-awareness promotes equity and a focus on the whole child.
18. School Leadership ____ Staff ____ realize they are ultimately responsible for leading trauma-awareness in the school/division.
19. School Leadership ____ Staff ____ realize the urgency for their leaders and staff to become trauma-aware.
20. School Leadership ____ Staff ____ realize the need and value of engaging families, community members, and students (at the secondary level) in the process of becoming trauma-aware.

TOTAL: School Leadership ____ Staff ____
    20-40 = *Spend significant PD time with your School Leadership/Staff on becoming trauma-aware.*
    41-50 = *Spend a moderate amount of PD time with School Leadership/Staff on becoming trauma-aware.*
    51-60 = *Your School Leadership/Staff is trauma-aware and ready to work on becoming trauma-sensitive.*

Appendix B
ACE Questionnaire

Prior to your 18th birthday:

1. Did a parent or other adult in the household often or very often... Swear at you, put you down, or humiliate you? or Act in a way that made you afraid that you might be physically hurt?

    No ____ If Yes, enter 1 ____

2. Did a parent or other adult in the household often or very often... Push, grab, slap, or throw something at you? or Ever hit you so hard that you had marks or were injured?

    No ____ if Yes, enter 1 ____

3. Did an adult or person at least 5 years older than you ever... Touch or fondle you or have you touch their body in a sexual way? or Attempt or actually have oral, anal, or vaginal intercourse with you?

    No ____ if Yes, enter 1 ____

4. Did you often or very often feel... No one in your family loved you or thought you were important or special? or Your family did not look out for each other, feel close to each other, or support each other?

    No ____ if Yes, enter 1 ____

5. Did you often or very often feel that ... You didn't have enough to eat, had to wear dirty clothes, and had no one to protect you? or Your parents were too drunk or high to take care of you or take you to the doctor if you needed it?

    No ____ if Yes, enter 1 ____

6. Were your parents ever separated or divorced?

    No ____ If Yes, enter 1 ____

7. Was your mother or stepmother often or very often pushed, grabbed, slapped, or had something thrown at her? or Sometimes, often or very often kicked , bitten, hit with a fist, or hit with something hard? or Ever repeatedly hit over at least a few minutes or threatened with a gun or knife?

    No ____ if Yes, enter 1 ____

8. Did you live with someone who was a problem drinker, or alcoholic, or who used street drugs?

    No ____ If Yes, enter 1 ____

9. Was a household member depressed or mentally ill, or did a household member attempt suicide?

    No ____ If Yes, enter 1 ____

10. Did a household member go to prison?

    No ____ It Yes, enter 1 ____

Now add up your "Yes" answers. This is your ACE score. _____

Appendix C
Devereux Adult Resilience Survey (DARS)

Take time to reflect and complete each item on the survey below. There are no right answers. Once you have finished, reflect on your strengths and then start small and plan for one or two things that you feel are important to improve.

		Yes	Sometimes	Not Yet
Relationships	1. I have good friends who support me.			
	2. I have a mentor or someone who shows me the way.			
	3. I provide support to others.			
	4. I am empathetic.			
	5. I trust my close friends.			
Internal Beliefs	1. My role as a caregiver is important.			
	2. I have personal strengths.			
	3. I am creative.			
	4. I have strong beliefs.			
	5. I am hopeful about the future.			
	6. I am lovable			
Initiative	1. I communicate effectively with those around me.			
	2. I try many different ways to solve a problem.			
	3. I have a hobby that I engage in.			
	4. I seek out new knowledge.			
	5. I am open to new ideas.			
	6. I laugh often.			
	7. I am able to say no.			
	8. I can ask for help.			
Self-Control	1. I express my emotions.			
	2. I set limits for myself.			
	3. I am flexible.			
	4. I can calm myself down.			

Appendix D
Strategic Vision Builder

_____ **(School) aspires to practice restorative vs. punitive student discipline.**

1. SAFETY
   a. What vision of ***safety*** will guide your school discipline? (**R**ecognize)
   b. What specific practices (missions) will help support this vision? (**R**espond)
   c. What staffing, support, and timeline of implementation will sustain and normalize these practices? (**R**esist)

2. CHOICE AND CONTROL
   a. What vision of ***choice and control*** will guide your school discipline? (**R**ecognize)
   b. What specific practices (missions) will support this vision? (**R**espond)
   c. What staffing, support, and timeline of implementation will sustain and normalize these practices? (**R**esist)

3. COLLABORATION
   a. What vision of ***collaboration*** will guide your school discipline? (**R**ecognize)
   b. What specific practices (missions) will help support this vision? (**R**espond)
   c. What staffing, support, and timeline of implementation will sustain and normalize these practices? (**R**esist)

4. TRUSTWORTHINESS
   a. What vision of ***trustworthiness*** will guide your school discipline? (**R**ecognize)
   b. What specific practices (missions) will help support this vision? (**R**espond)
   c. What staffing, support, and timeline of implementation will sustain and normalize these practices? (**R**esist)

5. EMPOWERMENT
   a. What vision of ***empowerment*** will guide your school discipline? (**R**ecognize)
   b. What specific practices (missions) will help support this vision? (**R**espond)
   c. What staffing, support, and timeline of implementation will sustain and normalize these practices? (**R**esist)

Appendix E
Restorative Justice Mindset Survey

Restorative justice is more than a program or practice, it is a mindset, a way of doing business and approaching our work everyday. A restorative mindset is driven by key values and concepts which are outlined below. Rank each statement using the scale provided.

I almost always have this mindset	I often have this mindset	I sometimes have this mindset	I rarely have this mindset	I almost never have this mindset

1. I place **relationships** at the center, recognizing that relationships are critical for making progress whether on large community issues or for an individual who is going through personal challenges.
2. I value **collaboration and collective voice**, recognizing that all peoples' voices are important and that we must have structures and protocols in place that engage all stakeholders rather than a few individuals, even in times of conflict.
3. I recognize that **communities** are responsible for the individuals in the community and vice versa. Restorative justice mindsets look to a community to solve its own challenges and support individuals in the community in healing and repairing harm they may have caused.
4. I acknowledge **multiple truths** and that each individual has a unique perspective which should be shared, honored, and heard.
5. I believe that **respectful dialogue** is possible in any given situation. While certain topics may cause tension or vulnerability, a Restorative Justice mindset believes that with the right space and values a respectful dialogue can take place.
6. I ask that individuals be **vulnerable** and willing to engage in honest conversations with others.
7. I ask individuals to be held **accountable** for their actions. This means that individuals should be able to acknowledge their role in any harm and take steps to repair any harm that they have caused.
8. I acknowledge that **healing** is a process and that is must take place after harm happens to individuals and/or communities. Without an appropriate healing process, additional harm may be caused.
9. I ask how conflicts and harm can be **restored** after they have taken place. The goal of restoration is to rebuild relationships, restore the communities and individuals after harm, and work with those who caused the harm to prevent a similar incident from happening in the future.
10. I believe that **constructive solutions** are always possible and work towards discovering those solutions together.

Index

Kotter, J. P. 3, 41–43, 45, 57–58, 75–76, 85, 101–102, 130, 131, 148

Loudoun County Public Schools (LCPS) 68–69, 91–93, 140–142

mental health 3, 10, 20, 26, 32, 41–43, 45–46, 48, 50, 52, 57–58, 66, 69–70, 75–76, 84, 91–92, 95, 101–102, 111–113, 116, 120, 130–137, 140–143, 148
mindfulness 36, 46, 117–118
Missouri Model 41–43, 75, 101, 130
multi-tiered systems of support (MTSS) 36, 51, 69, 111–113, 132–133, 138, 140, 142

neuroplasticity 33, 35–36

office discipline referral (ODR) 12, 83, 112, 114, 137

Positive Behavioral Interventions and Supports (PBIS) 36, 68–69, 91, 103, 111, 113–115, 116, 118, 122, 136, 142
poverty 3, 7, 14–18, 20, 28, 34, 40, 44, 60, 62, 64–65, 90, 107, 139
Principles of Trauma-Informed Care (TIC) 42, 75, 86

realize 3, 43–44, 57–58, 60–73, 92, 97, 101–102, 107, 113–114
recognize 3, 41, 43–44, 75–91, 93–96, 101–102, 107–108, 112–113, 116–117, 138, 143
reform 3–4, 40, 43–48, 51, 57–58, 76, 78, 86, 96, 101–102, 131, 148
resilience 1, 3–4, 20–21, 26, 33–36, 40, 45–47, 58–61, 70, 72, 75, 77–78, 83–88, 93, 96, 102–104, 106–107, 118, 136, 141–142, 148
resist 3, 31, 43–44, 52, 87, 130–132, 134–136, 140, 142–143
respond 3, 10, 36, 43–44, 62, 66, 71, 76, 83, 87–88, 94–96, 101–104, 108, 111, 121, 148
restorative in-school suspension 36, 119
restorative justice (RJ) 21, 36, 46, 50, 76, 93, 118–119
restorative practices (RP) 36, 46, 49, 51, 69, 70, 76, 90, 92, 118–119, 121–123, 138–139, 141–142

Richmond Public Schools (RPS) 45–46, 65, 93, 110, 117, 142
routines 36, 42, 44, 83, 101, 106, 114

safety 7, 28, 34, 35, 42, 50–51, 76–78, 86–87, 91, 104
school-to-prison pipeline 15–16, 137
secure attachment 33–36
sense of urgency 3, 41, 43–44, 57–58, 60–62, 101
social-emotional learning (SEL) 36, 46, 51, 62, 70, 92–93, 115–117, 132
Sources of Strength 92–93, 142
special education 13–14, 36, 67, 80, 89, 122, 133
strategic vision 41, 43, 75, 85–88, 101–102, 121, 131
students with disabilities (SWD) 11, 13, 15, 65, 69, 83, 90, 121, 136, 142
Substance Abuse and Mental Health Services Administration (SAMHSA) 3, 10, 41–43, 70, 101, 131, 148
suicide 20, 32–33, 69, 92, 141
sustain the momentum 130–131

Taylor Middle School 122
teaching discipline 3, 17, 104
toxic stress 21, 30
trauma-aware 42–43, 47, 57–59, 61–64, 67–70, 96
trauma-informed 3–4, 36, 41–43, 47, 52, 58–59, 61, 66–68, 71, 75, 80, 84–87, 93, 112, 122, 130–132, 134, 136–137, 139, 141, 143, 144, 148
Trauma-Informed Leadership Team (TILT) 58, 66–67, 143
trauma-responsive 3–4, 21, 26, 36, 40–48, 51–52, 62–63, 66, 70, 86–88, 93–96, 101–103, 107, 113, 116–117, 119, 130–132, 134, 143, 148
trauma-sensitive 42, 47, 75, 77, 79, 83, 86–88, 90, 95

Virginia Center for Inclusive Communities (VCIC) 71, 90, 95, 107
Virginia Tiered Systems of Supports (VTSS) 132–134

zero tolerance 7, 14–16, 48, 50, 58, 62–63